MR. AMERICANO

MR. AMERICANO

ADDISON ROSE

NEW DEGREE PRESS
COPYRIGHT © 2023 ADDISON ROSE
All rights reserved.

MR. AMERICANO

ISBN   979-8-88926-403-3 *Paperback*
           979-8-88926-405-7 *Hardcover*
           979-8-88926-404-0 *Ebook*

For my friends and family.

TABLE OF CONTENTS

A NOTE FROM THE AUTHOR	11
CHAPTER 1	15
CHAPTER 2	25
CHAPTER 3	33
CHAPTER 4	43
CHAPTER 5	53
CHAPTER 6	61
CHAPTER 7	73
CHAPTER 8	83
CHAPTER 9	93
CHAPTER 10	103
CHAPTER 11	111
CHAPTER 12	119
CHAPTER 13	131
CHAPTER 14	141
CHAPTER 15	149
CHAPTER 16	157
CHAPTER 17	163
CHAPTER 18	173
CHAPTER 19	181
CHAPTER 20	191
CHAPTER 21	199

CHAPTER 22	205
CHAPTER 23	217
CHAPTER 24	227
CHAPTER 25	239
CHAPTER 26	247
EPILOGUE	253
ACKNOWLEDGMENTS	257

*Don't get so busy making a living
that you forget to make a life.*

—DOLLY PARTON

A NOTE FROM THE AUTHOR

—

While it pains me to admit it now, there was a time in my life when I viewed reading as a chore. I considered it a mandatory task rather than a source of delight or pleasure.

It wasn't until my teenage years that I discovered it was possible to actually *enjoy* reading. Katie Klein's high school heartthrobs, the classics from Nicholas Sparks, and Mila Gray's emotional series on first loves changed my perspective completely. Thanks to them, reading evolved into one of my favorite pastimes and most significant influences. Turning the page became a thrill, allowing me to find friends in the characters and excitement in the storylines.

The more I read, the more I viewed storytelling as an art—something that can be inspirational, compelling, and persuasive. During my sophomore year of college, I found myself back in my hometown for spring break, curled up in my childhood bedroom with Jenna Evans Welch's *Love & Gelato* in hand. While I was initially bummed to be spending time with fictional characters rather than my real-life friends, it turned out to be a life-changing decision.

In awe of the protagonist's transformation and cultural experiences after spending the summer in Italy, I wanted to embark on my own journey of self-discovery. When I turned the last page around 2:00 a.m., I began my search for study abroad programs I could apply for immediately.

After weighing my options and receiving my parents' blessing, I proceeded to build my summer abroad bucket list, complete with museums to visit and gelato flavors to try. Two months later, I boarded a plane to Europe without knowing a soul and set out on the adventure of a lifetime—all because of a *book*.

While I love novels that take me to magical places and feature fairytale plot lines, I recognize they can be far from realistic. Because the truth is, growing up and falling in love doesn't look the same for everyone. It isn't always picture-perfect, but it is still beautiful.

Living in a world where it seems everyone else has it all *figured out*, I often have to remind myself there is no such thing as a perfect timeline or path to follow. I've come to learn there is no need to rush into the next phase of life, and the grass is not always greener on the other side. Just because *others* may be getting promoted, engaged, married, or becoming parents doesn't mean *you* are behind or need to do the same thing.

Success, happiness, and fulfillment do not come from copying others but rather from finding yourself and embracing the qualities that make *you* unique. When the time is right, love will come around and sweep you off your feet.

My favorite novels have always been those that captivate me from the start through either a relatable main character or a dreamy romance. So, when I decided to create *my* story, it was these two elements I was most determined to include.

Mr. Americano is inspired by the fantastic storytelling and touching romances from authors like Colleen Hoover, Christina Lauren, Josie Silver, and Emily Henry. Though this is a complete work of fiction, my writing was influenced by the phase of life I am in and many of the experiences young women in today's world share.

I hope you find *Mr. Americano* to be a lighthearted and relatable story that reminds you to reflect (try journaling!) and appreciate each phase of life for what it is, not what you want it to be. Remember, there is a reason for every season, and *the best is yet to come.*

Cheers to *adulting* and falling in love!

XOXO

CHAPTER 1

―――

Since the moment Margaret and Marshall met, they've been in love.

Her eyes fill with stars, and her stomach swarms with butterflies whenever he crosses her mind. She never thought she would be so lucky as to fall in love with a man who exceeds her wildest hopes and dreams. Her college sweetheart, no less.

She fondly remembers how he got down on one knee during a strategically planned graduation photoshoot in the spring of their senior year. The golden hour glow combined with freshly bloomed wildflowers in the background made it seem like a scene straight out of a movie. That was him, thinking of every single detail.

He had intentionally coordinated the whole day, and everyone except for Margaret was in on the plan. The photographer captured the moment beautifully, including Margaret's tears of joy, providing a series of photos to cherish forever.

The thought of walking down the aisle causes Margaret's eyes to fill with stars and her stomach with butterflies all over again—a feeling that has become all too familiar over the years they have spent together. He is honest, kind, charming, respectful, and driven. He's all Margaret has ever hoped for and more.

It's hard to believe that today is her wedding day. She has been dreaming of it forever, and it's finally here!

"Woof! Woof!"

Grudgingly, Margaret opens her eyes and rolls over to steal a peek at her phone, easing back into reality.

6:44 a.m.

Rubbing her temples, she contemplates pulling the covers over her head and pretending not to hear the repetitive woofs echoing down the hall. Any other time, she would protest the little dachshund's beckoning and avoid rewarding such behavior, but today, that isn't an option.

Despite reeling from the fact that Penelope Grace rudely interrupted her *perfect* dream, Margaret sluggishly falls out of bed anyway and slides on her trademark pair of UGG slippers. Making her way across the apartment in a daze, she dodges halfway unpacked U-Haul boxes along the way.

She hooks Penelope's turquoise leash to her matching collar, and they begin their morning jaunt around the apartment complex.

Tracing the perimeter of the neighboring building, Margaret observes the freshly trimmed shrubs and appreciates how the gentle fall breeze blows her bedhead hair off her shoulders.

Unsurprisingly, Penelope is adjusting nicely to San Antonio, making herself at home and claiming her new territory with pride. Margaret, on the other hand, is taking a little more time to get acclimated. The farther she gets from her college years, the more she realizes that they did not prepare her for what she is feeling now.

Lonely.

The pressure and responsibility of being on her own are proof that *adulting* isn't all it's cracked up to be.

Though it took five years, Margaret achieved her goal *and* met her parents' expectations of double majoring in marketing and strategic management. In addition to her degree, she walked away with countless memories and the best group of friends a girl could ask for.

Tugging on Penelope's leash to keep her moving, Margaret thinks back to her dream from this morning and frowns. Unlike her friends, the only people in the audience cheering during her five seconds of fame on the graduation stage were her parents. No boyfriend was down on one knee after the ceremony or fiancé beaming with pride. Needless to say, she did not receive a jaw-dropping emerald-cut diamond on a gold band, just a class ring engraved with her graduation year.

"Don't you love a plan? And a man with a plan?" Margaret asks Penelope Grace as she observes a couple from the building in front of them packing up their car for some fun-looking adventure. "Me too… but unfortunately, we don't have either at the moment, do we? I think I've given up on both." As they keep walking, Margaret continues talking. "What about you? Have you seen that little Chihuahua from the dog park again?"

Playful one-sided conversations are part of their new routine. Margaret talks a lot, and Penelope listens—interjecting the occasional bark. It works. *It's what you do when you live alone*, Margaret justifies.

Growing up, it's easy to have it all planned out… that is, in your head, at least. Finish high school, get into your dream college, meet the love of your life on day one, be engaged by senior year, marry by twenty-four, have kids by twenty-six, travel the world, and live happily ever after… blah blah blah.

"How in the world did we end up *here*, Penelope Grace?" she asks, wishing her little dog with a big personality could shed some wisdom on the topic. Instead, PG is far too preoccupied with the leaves tumbling across the grass and the faint bark of other dogs in the distance. Margaret trails behind her, doing her best to keep up and prevent the retractable leash from popping.

Rounding the corner of another building in their spacious, farmhouse-inspired complex, Margaret makes eye contact with a girl who also looks to be in her midtwenties. Feeling friendly, she waves and mumbles, "Good morning!" as the girl exits her vehicle, seemingly in a rush with full hands and a frantic face.

The petite blond wearing navy blue scrubs looks up with a kind, half smile. "Hi," she says before slamming the car door shut and shifting her gaze to Penelope Grace. "Oh my gosh, she's so cute! Can I pet her?"

Penelope squirms on the ground with her leash pulled taut, dying for a belly rub from the stranger.

"Of course," Margaret says, easing forward. "She clearly is *starving* for attention." Margaret rolls her eyes and gestures to Penelope, who has flopped onto her back, her stomach now on full display.

With her attention focused solely on the dog, the neighbor asks, "What's her name? Her color is beautiful!"

Margaret beams with pride as if she had control over the dog's picturesque black and tan dapple coat. "Thank you. Her name is Penelope Grace. Don't let her fool you. She's a handful," Margaret warns, her tone sincere and motherly.

"That's *so* cute! I love it!"

Margaret nods appreciatively. Then, digging deep for extra courage to capitalize on the opportunity to introduce herself too, she slips her hair behind her ear and adds, "And I'm Margaret, by the way." She shifts her weight from one foot to the other and tacks on, "We just moved in last week."

Her potential new friend stands, triggering Penelope to jump up and down, demanding more attention. "Welcome! I'm Britt. So nice to meet you both!" she says, glancing between Margaret and her four-legged counterpart.

"Likewise!" Margaret agrees, trying to match Britt's confidence and energy. They continue chatting until Penelope begins barking ferociously at a nearby pug and its owner. They take this as their cue to part ways and agree to catch up later.

Continuing along the concrete path, Margaret smiles. Having made her first local friend, she is now excited to be on her own, without her parents or roommates to account for, and eager to see what her new life in San Antonio has to offer.

* * *

Margaret's first Monday in Corporate America is a success! Although the pandemic resulted in an unfortunate two-year delay, she is a marketing professional, at last!

"Our professors would be so proud," she says to Penelope Grace while pouring herself a celebratory glass of wine.

Though it was an exciting first day on the job, it also felt rather anticlimactic. Margaret took PG outside a few times, only to return to the apartment like a boomerang. Her human interaction was limited to Zoom calls and neighborly waves, neither of which *actually* counted.

Sitting on her new, emerald-green velvet couch, the most *adult* purchase from her big move to the city, Margaret sips on her wine and admires her new feminine and chic space.

Bold, jewel-tone colors, and fun textures are sprinkled throughout. A few boxes and pieces of artwork linger along the walls, begging to be assigned to their new home. Her vision is gradually coming together, and all the hours she and her roommates spent watching HGTV shows in college are finally paying off! And although she is loving the outcome, Margaret already has her mind on *what's next*, always eager to move on to something bigger and better.

Inspired by one of her go-to podcasters known for touting the benefits of journaling and reflection, Margaret has finally decided to give it a try as part of her new city, new job, and new me mentality. Her legs crisscrossed and her brand-new journal in hand, Margaret contemplates how to best capture today's whirlwind of emotions in less than a paragraph.

She brainstorms a few different approaches...

> *I started my new job today and felt everything from excitement to nausea before noon. I'm excited about the future and not feeling like the new girl anymore. Yay for finally chasing my dreams and living in the city! :)*

Or

> *Day one in the books. Paycheck coming soon! Whoop! My mentor, Amanda, seems super cool and fun. I have a feeling she's going to teach me a lot, and we might even become besties! Celebrating day one with a glass (or three) or vino. :'-)*

Or

> *I can't decide how I feel. Equal parts excited and terrified about growing up. I started my job today, and I feel underqualified. I'm happy to be here in my own place but also feeling homesick... I'm a little worried that growing up isn't quite all it's cracked up to be. :/*

But none of them feel quite right.

Overwhelmed, Margaret puts the pen down and retrieves her favorite Snickers-flavored ice cream from the freezer, her go-to solution for all of life's problems. She can say no to cookies, cakes, pies, and pastries, but turning down ice cream is *never* in the cards.

Not long after, she plops down with the carton and a spoon, Penelope brings over a toy for fetch, and Margaret's mom calls.

"Hey, honey! How was your first day? I want to hear all about it!"

Multi-tasking between tossing the plush, faux Louis Vuitton down the hallway and answering her mother's questions, Margaret allows herself to relax.

"It was good. I think I'm really gonna like this girl named Amanda on my team. And my boss, Lacey, seems nice too," Margaret says, aiming to give her mom just enough information to appease her.

"That's great to hear! You get along well with everybody, so I'm not surprised one bit."

Swallowing an oversized bite of ice cream and chucking the toy as far as she can, Margaret mumbles, "It was a little boring being at home, though." Her voice dips down, her disappointment evident.

"You'll be going into the office some, right? Do you have a schedule?"

"Yes, I'm going in tomorrow," Margaret confirms. "We have a rough schedule, but it sounds flexible. Probably a few days a week."

"Oh, wonderful! I hope you have a cute outfit picked out," she says in a motherly tone.

Margaret rolls her eyes as if her mother has forgotten she's twenty-six years old and can properly dress herself. "Got it, Mom. Don't worry." Her tone is sharper than before, but she tries to let it go, knowing her mom means well.

"I'm just saying first impressions matter is all. You can't be looking like a slob now," she cautions.

Though she hasn't always been a fan of her mom's interrogations and warnings, the familiarity of the moment is exactly what she needs.

Eventually, they wrap up the conversation and agree to talk again tomorrow, leaving Margaret where she started, struggling to sum up the day. Glancing over at one of the many group photos on display in her new home, she can't help but pause and wonder what the entries of her three closest friends might read today.

TESS: *Cooked dinner for my husband! Snuggled up on the couch and rewatched our wedding video! Can't believe it's already been six months of marriage <3*

CAROLINE: *The wedding is less than two months away! Picked up my dress after my final fitting and*

> met with the florist today! So ready to be a wife! Mrs. Johnson, coming right up!
>
> SUSANNAH: *Still can't believe I'm going to be a mom! It's starting to feel real now that all my friends and family know. So excited to start decorating the nursery and experience parenthood with Steven!*

It's almost laughable how different their lives are today, yet how similar they were just a couple of years ago.

Margaret has to imagine their past entries went a little something like…

> TGIF! The girls and I enjoyed our weekly four-hour dinner, complete with three bottles of wine, two apps, and four desserts. We laughed uncontrollably, planned our futures, and reminisced on our favorite college memories. Love them!

Although it doesn't feel like too long ago, and the group could likely pick up where they left off, things are different now. Dinners must be planned three months in advance, at least one person will have to travel more than four hours, and the majority of the group has to coordinate plans with a *spouse*. Margaret, of course, has to plan around Penelope Grace, but considering she's practically a traveling companion, it's hardly a deterrent.

The point is that times change. And that's okay. *Change isn't always bad,* Margaret reminds herself, eager for the next chapter of her life, despite the loneliness and fear of being "behind" creeping in.

Without overthinking it any further, she settles on her first entry…

> *A super successful day one as a working woman! Feeling accomplished and proud of myself for taking this leap, despite the unknowns. Can't wait to make some new friends and make this place feel like home. I can do this!*

Longing for extra comfort and company to combat her loneliness, Margaret gives Penelope special privileges to forgo her kennel. Trotting off to bed, Margaret smiles and replays six keywords of her first entry—*make this place feel like home.*

CHAPTER 2

"Hi, Lucy!" Margaret exclaims, greeting her favorite barista at The Brew. Though they only met a couple of weeks ago, they bonded instantly over their favorite reality TV shows and Lucy's San Antonio must-sees.

In her late teens, Lucy is working here to pay her way through school. With a choppy haircut and purple highlights, she's unlike Margaret's other friends, but it works. She has been friendly and welcoming, and that's all Margaret can ask for.

"Good afternoon, lady," Lucy says, her quirky personality peeking through. "What can I get ya on this fine Thursday? The usual?"

Margaret nods and smiles, her tastebuds craving yet another iced americano. Despite having been to The Brew less than a dozen times, Lucy seems to have caught on quickly.

Lucy's hand hovers above the different cup options as she eyes Margaret over the top of her trendy tortoise glasses.

"Let's make it a large. I need all the caffeine I can get to finish this workday," Margaret says, having come to The Brew with a lengthy to-do list and in need of a scenery change.

The espresso aficionado retrieves the appropriate cup and scribbles barista gibberish on the side.

Margaret analyzes the fresh pastry assortment behind the bar, her stomach grumbling for sustenance. "Can I add a blueberry scone too? They look delicious!"

Her order placed, Margaret heads to a small, semi-hidden table she discovered on her first visit, passing other patrons working, chatting, and studying along the way. Tucked in the corner, it became her favorite spot because the sunrays spill in beautifully, the music is slightly less obnoxious, and she is less likely to be disturbed. Also, it doesn't make for a distracting Zoom background should she be called into *yet another* impromptu meeting.

She situates herself and her work area—laptop, notepad, to-do list, and headphones on display. Glancing in the direction of the bar, she notices her drink patiently waiting to be claimed. Already in "the zone," Margaret beelines over to the pickup station.

Midreach, her hands graze, and her arms tangle with a stranger.

It takes her a second to remove her lanky limbs from the mix-up. "Why are you trying to steal my energy?"

Confused and silent, he furrows his brow.

As his expression gradually comes into focus, Margaret realizes her last statement, courtesy of her caffeine-deprived brain, likely made little sense.

Embarrassing.

"My coffee," she clarifies, running her free hand through her hair in frustration. "Why were you trying to steal my coffee?"

Stammering, the tall, tan, and handsome stranger responds, "I, uh, think it's actually *my* coffee…" His eyes dart from Margaret to the coffee in question to the barista behind the counter and back again.

His deep voice and perfect posture almost take her breath away. Sporting business casual attire custom-fit for his masculine frame, the mystery man's presence makes it feel like the walls are closing in. Margaret struggles to think clearly, and her judgment is clouded due to his presence.

Because it is in her nature to apologize any time she slightly inconveniences someone, even if accidental or faultless, Margaret whispers, "Oh, sorry…" She fidgets with her shoulder-length hair again and wishes she could just disappear.

Taking a second to breathe and collect herself, Margaret does a little shimmy to loosen up and pry her gaze from his piercing blue eyes. His hair is effortlessly styled, and the color is somewhere between an amber and brown ale beer. How dare he look so handsome after just depriving her of her caffeine?

I want to love him and hate him all at the same time.

Margaret notices his weight shifting and his eyes studying every inch of her while other coffee drinkers buzz around, retrieving their beverages without incident like ordinary people. For a moment, it feels like life is happening all around them and they are frozen in time. Nothing seems to matter. Except *him.*

His cheeks pinch and reveal a small dimple as he finally speaks again. "Ha. Sorry… It's an iced americano…" he says, holding the cup up in the air to reveal its dark, espresso color. He glances between Margaret and the dairy, sugar, and fix-up station located to the side with insinuation. "Not exactly what I thought you would order," he adds.

Margaret struggles to discern his tone—somewhere between flirty, cocky, and downright arrogant, none of which sit right with her.

She stands with her arms akimbo and tries to hide her defensiveness. "Your point?"

Shaking his head and finally cracking a full smile, Mr. Americano steps away, letting Margaret's unnecessarily sassy words hang in the air.

His model-worthy grin makes her knees wobble, so she places a hand on the cold, concrete countertop, and exhales, waiting for her *actual* order to be placed up for grabs.

Despite Mr. Americano being out of sight, Margaret is suddenly self-conscious of her three-day-old hair, wrinkled T-shirt, and favorite pair of old joggers. She wishes she would have upped her attire and invested a little more in her appearance before leaving the house this morning as her mom's voice echoes in her ear. She crosses her arms with a huff to cover up and hide her laziness.

Positioned awkwardly by the bar, Margaret wonders about his story. His name? *That would be nice to know. Why didn't I think to look at his cup?* Lucy is always so good about double-checking her visitors' names and spelling.

Missed opportunity.

"Iced americano and a blueberry scone for Margaret! Ready at the counter!" Lucy's counterpart calls out.

Grabbing her fix and smiling gratefully, she saunters back over to her corner table and tucks her head down behind her laptop screen, attempting to achieve invisibility. Margaret regrets sitting at her usual table and wishes for once she had been spontaneous.

Another missed opportunity.

Perhaps they would be sharing a table, clinking their biodegradable cups together, and sipping strong coffee with locked eyes. Margaret might know more than his coffee order by now and be making plans to see him again. As she takes a sip, her mind wants to continue down this rabbit hole of what-ifs. Instead, she wills it to stop and snaps the cup back down on the table with great triumph.

Despite her lengthy to-do list, the only thing Margaret is interested in accomplishing is learning more about Mr. Americano.

Margaret makes a pact with herself to at least clear out her email inbox before looking up again. Her new role as a marketing associate involves a good mix of internal and external communication. Still getting her bearings and familiarizing herself with projects, responding to even one message is a daunting task. Her mentor, Amanda, promises it will get easier, but "it just takes time."

She doesn't even make it through two email client inquiries before being paralyzed by a deep, masculine voice. "Margaret, was it?"

Her heart plummets. The intoxicatingly handsome, coffee-stealing man is towering over her and knows her *name*. Margaret shifts in her seat, hyper-aware of her surroundings, her appearance, and his presence.

The butterflies from their earlier encounter buzz with renewed energy. Her palms damp and her heart racing, Margaret drums her fingers along the table and searches for the words to properly address him. Just as she opens her mouth to speak, an incoming call on the Microsoft Teams app interrupts her train of thought.

Damn you, impromptu video calls.

Glancing between the screen and the most attractive man she's ever seen, Margaret is at a crossroads.

Considering it is only day nine on the job, Margaret is not exactly at the point in her career where she can afford to decline calls from her boss in favor of talking to sexy strangers.

With a disheartened but understanding look, Mr. Americano nods and says, "Take it," already turning on his heels and retreating to the well-loved leather chair he had emerged from. With a shrug, Margaret tries to find the silver lining—at least now she knows where he's sitting.

Stuffing her headphones back into her ears, rolling her eyes, and clicking *accept*, Margaret can't help but fear she let something special slip through her fingers.

"Hey, Margaret!" Lacey says. With over two decades of agency and client experience, Lacey leads their midsize team with intelligence, understanding, and flexibility—their hybrid work schedule being a prime example. So far, Margaret likes her.

She gets straight to the point. "How is week two going? Is Amanda showing you the ropes?"

The rest of the team gradually pops up on the screen, their audio and video connecting in a contagion. "I'm making it," Margaret says honestly, her mind still elsewhere. "Amanda has been great!"

"I know learning so much so fast can be overwhelming, so don't stress yourself out about anything… Yet, at least!" Lacey adds with a wink.

"Hey, team!" Amanda chirps, her video appearing on screen and revealing her perfectly curled hair and made-up face. Every time Margaret has interacted with Amanda, she has been dressed to the nines like a celebrity prepared to walk the red carpet. Meanwhile, Margaret takes full advantage of their work-from-home days and casual standards.

But maybe I should be like more Amanda. Margaret glances down at her clothes which have most definitely seen their better days.

"Margaret, I'm so sorry I didn't send you this invite sooner!" Amanda apologizes. "I thought it was already on your calendar, but I should've double-checked anyway. I'm glad you were able to hop on!"

Margaret nods politely but internally rolls her eyes in annoyance.

As the small talk fizzles out, Lacey takes charge of the conversation and conducts an efficient, albeit unexpected, team touch-base. Collecting status updates from Amanda and the other project leads on the team, Lacey probes deeper and makes recommendations as needed.

Margaret alternates between taking notes, acknowledging via nods, and daydreaming about Mr. Americano. When she has a chance to look up, his chair is *empty*. A twinge of sadness and regret pierce her chest.

"Margaret, can you present the proposal on Monday?" Lacey asks, jolting her back to the present.

What proposal? Which client? Shit.

Fumbling around for the unmute button and trying to buy herself time, Margaret nods vigorously. "Yes! Of course. I'll look for time on the calendar to discuss and prepare in advance. Thank you!" she says in the most poised and professional tone she can fake, truthfully having no idea what she just agreed to.

Scribbling down what she can on her notepad, Margaret searches for context clues on what she missed for the remainder of the conversation.

When the opportunity to click "leave meeting" finally presents itself, Margaret does so forcefully. Anxious to take a breather and mentally process all that just happened, she snaps her laptop shut and exhales audibly with her head hanging limply in her hands.

Thoughts swirling in her head, Margaret decides to indulge in her scone and sneak a peek in Mr. Americano's direction, hoping to see if he has returned from the restroom or with a refill. To her dismay, his seat is now occupied by a toddler climbing all over his mom, demanding another cake pop loud enough for the entire coffee shop to hear.

Dammit.

Because her workspace and lap are covered in crumbs, Margaret reaches for the only napkin in sight. She dusts off her laptop and the area in front of her before noticing something isn't quite right.

Hope and anticipation build inside of her as she discovers *more* than just The Brew logo printed on the napkin. She takes in the all-caps penmanship and stark black ink. The sight reminds her of a typewriter. Precise but oozing with personality.

> *Timing's never been my thing. Maybe we can try again?*

Though nameless, the brief note is concluded with his *phone number.*

Oh. My. Gosh.

CHAPTER 3

Still on cloud nine from the events that transpired in the coffee shop this afternoon, Hayes Thompson navigates his way through the airport crowd to the front of the Priority Boarding line for Gate 3. With his second coffee of the day in hand, he imagines what it would be like to travel with *her*. *Walking hand in hand through the terminal, sharing overpriced snacks, and arguing over who gets which seat...*

Shaking off the daydream, he rubs the back of his neck and lets his head hang, the muscles tight and tense. Throwing back the last of his drink, he tosses the cup in the trash bin just as his boarding pass is scanned.

It has been years since the mere sight of a woman has made him starry-eyed or nervous. While his friends and brothers have tried to set him up with various women over the years, dating has never been a priority for Hayes. He has agreed to a casual dinner here and there to appease them, but it's never gone any further.

Though he knows nothing more than her name and coffee order, Hayes is bound and determined to see Margaret again. Something about her is too intriguing to resist.

Walking down the jetway, he thinks about her natural beauty, from the shades of brown in her hair and eyes to her subtle makeup and casual, understated attire. She captivated him from the moment she walked into The Brew. While he wishes he could take credit for their drink mix-up rendezvous, that was just fate.

After shoving his belongings in the overhead bin and undoing the top button of his dress shirt, Hayes settles into his preferred aisle seat on the exit row. More appreciative than ever for the extra legroom, Hayes finally releases the built-up tension he has been harboring. Travel days are always a whirlwind, and while the chaos makes the time pass quickly, it is exhausting.

Preparing for the two-and-a-half-hour flight to Chicago, Hayes scrolls through his phone for a podcast that piques his interest while the flight attendant gives her safety spiel. Hayes is always on overdrive, and the thought of wasting time sitting still has never felt right. So, even during "downtime," he strives for productivity.

Settling on a new episode about leadership styles and career development, he clicks play and attempts to focus on something other than the striking and apparently feisty, average-height brunette already on his mind.

Forty-five minutes later, the recording concludes with four key takeaways, which Hayes jots down in the Notes app on his phone. Soon due for a promotion from senior consultant to partner, he hopes the nuggets of information will contribute to his next career advancement. While he may or may not *actually* reference them later, it's the thought that counts.

Since joining the firm almost eight years ago, Hayes has been aiming for the title of partner, working tirelessly to support his teams and clients. Shawn, his boss, has supported him since day one, seeing his potential and keeping track of his progress even when Hayes can't.

Working overtime on the weekends in different cities and countries hasn't always been easy or *fun,* but it is *finally* paying off. And while the hope of an upcoming promotion justifies the stress, lack of sleep, and abysmal social life, something about the day's events makes him wonder if there's still *more* to experience.

On autopilot, Hayes retrieves his belongings from baggage claim and finds his way to the ride-share pickup area, glancing at his watch and acclimating to the time change.

10:24 p.m.

Knowing his parents are likely awaiting his arrival, he provides them with a voluntary update.

> HAYES
> *Just landed! A little ahead of schedule. See you in 30ish.*

Walking with purpose but longing for food and sleep, Hayes keeps his eyes peeled for a red Toyota Camry.

Other than a quick, confirming, "Hayes?" as he opens the Camry door, the Uber driver remains silent for the duration of the ride and keeps the music turned down to slightly above a whisper. Hayes is left alone with his thoughts *again* for the drive across town. To his dismay, he can only think about Margaret—like a teenage boy crushing on a cute girl from math class.

What is she doing? Has she thought about me? I wonder what else we have in common.

He tries to suppress these questions, drumming up thoughts about work and impending deadlines. Under normal circumstances, this would do the trick. In fact, it is usually turning *off* this inner dialogue that is the struggle, not turning it on.

Motivated by his desire to see her again, Hayes reaches for his phone before remembering the unfortunate reality that gave him no choice but to leave *her* his number rather than the other way around. As the car pulls up to his parents' house, he shoves the phone back into his pocket and grabs his belongings. Taking his frustration out on the trunk, he slams it shut just as his phone chimes with an incoming message. *What if?*

With his hands full and parents waiting to greet him with arms opened wide on the front porch, now isn't the time to find out.

"Hi, honey! It's so good to see you!" his mom, Emma, chirps with excitement despite his late arrival. Though her cheeks are hollower and her hair is thinner these days, she still looks as put together as ever.

"Hey, Mom. How are you feeling?" Hayes asks, dropping his bag to the ground to give her a proper hug. "And hi, Dad," he adds, shaking his father's hand and reaching for a partial embrace. Hayes undoubtedly gets his height from his father. While his posture has changed over the years and caused him to lose a few inches, Jim is still well over six feet tall and wins every arm wrestle he's challenged to.

"I'm doing all right," Emma manages, hardly taking a breath. "Better now that you're here and not traveling among all those crazies." The trio walks through the threshold of the modest 1970s post-and-beam home, the original hardwood floors creaking beneath their feet. "Can I get you something to eat? Or drink? You look like you could use a pick-me-up."

While Hayes felt lucky to have her as his mom growing up, he has come to appreciate her much more as he's gotten older. She has always been as welcoming and hospitable as she could be, regardless of the circumstances.

Grateful for the offer, he nods appreciatively. "Yes, please, Mom. Whatever you have." Glancing around the kitchen for inspiration, he throws around a few suggestions. "Leftovers, a sandwich, eggs… I'll eat anything, and I can fix it. I really don't mind." He pauses a beat before sensing her impending protests. "You need to rest. Don't worry about taking care of me."

Hayes recognizes comments like that are a slippery slope these days, but he pushes the envelope anyway, willing to do anything to prove he cares about her as much as she cares about him.

Unsurprisingly, though, she takes control of the situation and instructs him to sit.

Comfortable and relaxed, Hayes observes his mother move effortlessly through the kitchen while he makes small talk with his dad.

"Did you see the game Monday night?" his dad asks, ever the football guru.

"I didn't watch the whole thing, but I caught the replays. Way too many penalties, and the missed field goals are inexcusable." Hayes shakes his head and intentionally adds fuel to his father's fire.

His dad spouts off various accompanying statistics related to the season before eventually changing the subject. "Emma, could you hand me some Advil from the cupboard? My head is pounding again."

"You bet, hun. Just a minute," Emma says, placing a full plate of meatloaf and mashed potatoes in front of Hayes before turning to dig through the medicine cabinet.

"Wow! I lucked out tonight!" Hayes's tone is dripping with sarcasm. He knows his mother well enough to know these are not leftovers. She *intentionally* doubled the recipe, knowing he would arrive starving.

She is an angel. Taking care of everyone else despite her own condition. How will we ever make it without her?

As he eats, he reflects on how little has changed about his parents' home over the years. The walls still hold family portraits from twenty-plus years ago. The floors feature the same old scuff marks from his dad's work boots. A gardenia-scented candle burns in the entryway, and the aroma drifts airily from room to room.

While the lack of change in their lives and routines has been a source of frustration for Hayes in the past, these moments make him appreciate their consistency. The familiarity now provides a sense of comfort rather than disdain. His life is blossoming into something completely different from theirs, more transient than stationary and more career than family oriented, but he's reminded at this moment to embrace *balance.*

"How was work this week? Busy as always, I assume?" his mom asks, her back to him as she tidies the kitchen towels and wipes off the counters.

"Oh, you know, the usual. We had some productive meetings and others that were a waste of time. Even still, I think the project is going well and might wrap up earlier than expected. That always means good things for me," Hayes says, already brainstorming how he might spend his bonus.

"You've always been a go-getter, H," his mom replies with pride. "I'm so glad we've been able to see more of you here lately. Your brothers are in and out all the time, you know. We miss you being closer."

Hayes is distracted by her fingers dancing along the countertop, one of her new ticks, and a side effect of the most recent medication added to her regimen. He nods, appreciating her praise and acknowledging the underlying message. *We want you here more.*

After washing his dishes, Hayes meanders down the narrow hallway to his childhood bedroom, subconsciously taking in the framed photos hung chronologically along the walls. Annual family photos, school yearbook pictures, and candid snapshots seem to capture every noteworthy life event.

Hayes and his brothers, Wes and Sam, have always had a good relationship despite the four-year gap between them. Though Hayes idolized Wes from day one, their age difference has always put them in opposing life stages, making it difficult sometimes to find common ground and empathy for one another.

Today, Wes lives in the Chicago suburbs with his wife, Lara, and three daughters. A foreign pang of jealousy washes over him as he observes the picturesque family of five in a brand-new gold frame.

While Hayes and Sam, his middle brother, once butted heads on everything, the unfortunate circumstances of recent years have brought them back together. Like Wes, Sam still lives close to home with his expecting wife. Another typical suburban family.

Being an uncle is as close to parenthood as Hayes has ever considered. The responsibility of raising his *own* children has never quite appealed to him.

Rounding the corner and flipping on the light switch, Hayes takes in the familiar, homey sight. While his baseball-themed bedding has arguably seen its better days, it's soft and cozy atop the new pillow-top mattress his parents recently purchased for the room. Iridescent trophies are stacked along his bookshelf, threatening to topple over if even slightly nudged, and outdated White Sox roster posters are plastered along the walls. The room reminds him of a time machine, transporting all who enter back to the nineties.

Shedding his stiff work clothes and crawling into bed, Hayes inhales and exhales slowly. His body aches from the long day, and his mind is eager to rest and recoup. Alone again, every inch of his body longs for more of Margaret. The thought of her serves as a reminder of the lonesome text tone from earlier.

>MARGARET
>*Hello, Mr. Americano. Apologies for earlier... Raincheck?*

Clever. With his cheeks a few degrees warmer now, Hayes attempts to type out an equally witty and flirtatious response without appearing too eager.

I'm so out of practice.

Unsatisfied with each string of words he puts together, he tosses the phone to the other side of the bed and flops over onto his stomach, his face now in the pillow. Whether an excuse to get to sleep faster or a desire to make the most positive impression possible, Hayes concludes sending a text this late at night might give the wrong idea.

Closing his eyes, Hayes mentally builds his to-do list for the following day.

1. Text Margaret
2. Take Mom to her appointments
3. Laundry
4. Follow-up on all work emails from today
5. Work out

By task five, he's already drifted off to sleep and begun to dream... While a relationship is *not* in the cards for Hayes, companionship *might* be...

CHAPTER 4

Despite sending what she thought was the *perfect* message, Margaret's phone remains silent.

Dry as the desert.

Even now, more than twelve hours later.

Determined not to let Mr. Americano's lack of communication get her down, Margaret goes about her Friday with poise and confidence, eager to celebrate surviving two weeks of Corporate America after the workday concludes.

Because she will be spending today "in office" with Amanda, prepping for her big debut on Monday, Margaret finds it only fair to allow Penelope Grace a few extra minutes outside this morning. While there is no doubt PG appreciates the uninterrupted nap time, Margaret suffers from "mom guilt." Sure, it's only a few days a week, *but still.*

While completing their usual loop, Margaret sees Britt again for the first time since their initial encounter last week. The sight of her neighbor, once again sporting a navy scrub set, sparks a smile.

"Hey, Britt!" Margaret yells, immediately self-conscious of her volume.

The feeling dissipates when Britt returns the greeting with equal enthusiasm, despite the fact it is barely after 7 a.m. "Hey, girl! How's it going?"

Margaret saunters across the parking lot with Penelope in tow, bringing their conversation to a more appropriate volume. "No complaints here, and yourself?"

"Other than just finishing my fourth night shift in a row, all is well with me, too," Britt says with an eye roll. "I *need* a nap."

Amazed, Margaret raises a brow. "The night shift? I can't imagine! What are your hours?" she inquires, this revelation explaining why she hasn't seen much of her bubbly neighbor.

"Lately, I've been working seven to seven. Sometimes I'm able to get off a little early, but it's brutal."

"I literally don't know how you do it," Margaret says, thinking about her regular 9:30 p.m. bedtime and the minimum eight hours of sleep she requires to function.

Chuckling in an I've-heard-that-before way, Britt says, "Honestly, me either. But I have the next couple of days off, and I can't wait to just chill."

"Would you maybe want to meet up for a happy hour after work or hang out this weekend?" Margaret asks nervously, craving more in person interaction and a girlfriend to talk about yesterday's encounter.

Before Margaret even has a chance to overthink her question, Britt agrees. "I would love that! I need something to make me feel like I have a normal life!"

Having left her phone on the charger, Margaret recites her number as Britt creates a new contact. "I'll shoot you a text, so you have my number too. We can connect later on the deets!"

With a pep in her step, Margaret guides Penelope back inside to prepare for the day. Unhooking the leash, she hears her phone ding across their shoebox-sized apartment. Presuming it's just Britt sharing her contact info as promised, Margaret continues with her morning routine.

After brewing a fresh cup of coffee, filling Penelope's food bowl, and watering her plants, she finally retrieves her phone.

She freezes in her tracks at the sight of the words *Mr. Americano* on her screen. Her heart pounds in her chest with anticipation.

Anxious to open the unread message, Margaret runs through several scenarios, preparing herself for the worst. She takes a deep breath before sliding up on the screen to learn her fate.

> MR. AMERICANO
> *Margaret, apologies for the delayed response.*

He's so polite and formal.

> MR. AMERICANO CONT.
> *I had a long day traveling and didn't want you to get the wrong idea by a late-night text.*

Love the humor.
Note to self—use travel as a discussion point.

> MR. AMERICANO CONT.
> *So, I decided to text you first thing this morning instead. :)*

A smiley face? Is he flirting? Or am I delirious?

Oh. My. Gosh. I don't even know where to start.

Already rushing to make it to the office on time, Margaret has no choice but to make him wait.

She does her best to be in the moment and soak up everything Amanda does and says all day. But instead of focusing on her mentor, Margaret is focused on *him*.

After referencing every deck, she can find in the archives, Margaret deems herself prepared for her presentation on Monday. Off the clock and able to succumb to her thoughts of Mr. Americano—*I hate that I'm still calling him that, but what else am I gonna call him?* She makes an effort to respond to his message. Rereading it again leaves her equally as flustered and curious as before. *Damn.*

> MARGARET
> *How thoughtful! Where are you? What's on your agenda this weekend?*

She hits send before second-guessing it and closes the app hastily when three little dots pop up. By the time she gets back home, a message awaits her.

> MR. AMERICANO
> *Booked today and tomorrow, but free Sunday night?*

Pleased with his proposal, Margaret obliges.

> MARGARET
> *Popular guy. Pencil me in for Sunday?*

MR. AMERICANO
My pleasure :) Let me know if you have any ideas... if not, I'll come up with something.

A man with a plan? Count me in!

Pacing around her bedroom, Margaret attempts to craft a quick response. Feeling pressured to pick out an appropriate "going-out" top in the next five minutes, she decides to make him wait again and resolves to text back later.

At 6:00 p.m. on the dot, Margaret meets Britt outside their apartment complex, where they are picked up by their first Uber driver of the evening.

Right off the bat, Britt engages in casual conversation that reminds Margaret of her college roommates and best friends. Despite this being their first time hanging out, it feels easy and natural. Like time with friends *should* feel.

It's nice to be able to chat with someone and not feel so alone.

Britt, a Fred's Bar frequenter, leads them through a sea of tables with striped umbrellas sprouting out of them. Margaret regrets her choice of an open-toed sandal as rocks pierce her feet but takes her time admiring the scenery anyway.

Fred's, located closer to Downtown than Margaret typically ventures, appears to be just her kind of place. Picnic tables scatter the vast patio, and live music sounds from inside. Fans and misters blow from above to combat the warm September temperatures, and patrons fan themselves with laminated copies of the happy hour menu.

Scanning the individuals at each table along their path, Margaret cannot help but think of her friends again. This would make the perfect place for a three-hour dinner with Tess, Susannah, and Caroline.

We should come here when, or if, they come to visit.

Settling down at a high-top table with a perfect view, Margaret peruses the menu. "What's your go-to drink? Anything in particular here that you recommend?"

"I'm usually a wine gal, but they have great cocktails here… The frosé is amazing if you're into that sort of thing," she advises. "I'm normally not much of a frozen fan, but it is absolutely delicious!"

Uninterested in reading any further, Margaret says, "Say no more! I'm in!"

Stacking their menus and folding her hands on the table, Britt leans in and says, "So… tell me everything!"

Seriously, how does she always have so much energy?

"Ha!" Margaret chuckles, self-conscious and not used to being the center of attention. "I don't even know where to start!"

"Okay, so I know you just moved here, but why? Let's start there."

Appreciating the guidance, Margaret wills herself to open up. Scanning the patio for their waiter and frosé, she says, "Well, I just got a new job, and I relocated so I could be in person at least some of the time."

Britt raises her eyebrows, clearly wanting more info. Margaret's posture weakens, and she takes her cue to elaborate. "I work in the marketing department of a local company. I'm an account manager, so I help different clients manage various projects and initiatives! Still learning the ropes but loving it so far."

"Amazing! I love it!"

She was totally a cheerleader growing up.

"What about you? How long have you lived in San Antonio?" Margaret asks, equally curious about her new blond bestie.

"I grew up here, went to college, then came back. Not exactly what I had planned, but it's where I got a job, so I didn't have a choice," she says with a shrug and an eye roll.

Gently banging her fist on the table for emphasis, Margaret agrees, feeling validated for the first time in forever. "Ugh! I know! I had to move home after graduation because my work plans completely fell through due to COVID-19. I worked at a boutique in my hometown until I got this job. Cute and fun, but so glad to be out."

They exchange stories about their parents and cheers their frosé to living alone and embracing change. "To adulting!" They clink.

Taking a sip of the frozen pink goodness, Britt says, "I take it you don't know many people in the area?"

"Just you," Margaret says with a sharp nod. "And my coworkers, but I'm not sure they count." She takes a sip of her drink, appreciating the refreshing temperature.

Suffering from a brain freeze, Britt makes a funny face and urges Margaret to continue.

"All of my friends spread out after graduation. And they are either already or about to be married," Margaret explains, attempting to disguise her jealousy with an upbeat tone.

Sighing, Britt sympathizes. "Girl, I feel you. It seems like I go to a wedding every weekend!" she exaggerates playfully. "I love a good excuse to dress up and see my friends, though, so I don't really mind."

"Same!" Margaret agrees. "One of my closest friends is actually getting married not far from here next month."

"Oh Em Gee! So fun!" Britt perks up and motions to their waiter for another round. "Tell me more! I assume you're in it?"

"Yep," Margaret confirms with pursed lips. "Bridesmaid duties ensue. I'm excited. It's at The Bella Hotel, which I haven't been to, but I've heard it is fab—"

"It is *stunning!* I'm so jealous!" Britt says with jazz hands. "Bachelorette party plans?"

Britt, eager to hear every detail, continues with the probing questions. But eventually, when she gets the chance, Margaret turns the conversation around, interested in learning more of Britt's story and seeing if she is the only one struggling with these thoughts and life-stage discrepancies.

Britt shares about her college experience, older sister, and guys she has casually dated. Anticipating what's next, Margaret's cheeks warm involuntarily.

"Are you dating anyone?" Britt asks innocently, slurping up the last of her cocktail.

Clearing her throat, Margaret manages to say no, but her beet-red face says otherwise.

Britt scrutinizes her with squinted eyes. "I feel like there's something you aren't sharing, missy." She adds a *tsk tsk* finger motion to further her disappointment.

Margaret attempts to shield her face and fan herself simultaneously.

"Spill!" Britt demands, her arms crossed like a parent who just caught their teenage kid red-handed.

Huffing, Margaret concurs. "I'm not seeing anyone. I just met someone. Yesterday." She leans forward for emphasis. "And he was *dreamy*."

Britt oohs and ahhs, demanding all the details—including access to Margaret's text messages. Once she is up to speed, they work together to craft a message back to him.

Giggling, they toss around ideas, ranging from serious to flirtatious to raunchy, before eventually agreeing on the *perfect balance.*

CHAPTER 5

MARGARET
Any plan that involves you and me sounds like an excellent plan to me;)

"Hayes, seriously? What's up with the childish grin on your face? You look like Candace after she's snuck a cookie or two without my knowing," Wes, the eldest of the brother trio, teases.

Hayes snaps his head up and shoves his phone back into his pocket, having reread the text from Margaret at least three times now and still struggling to respond. Refocusing on the TV featuring the first of many football games for the day, he chooses to ignore his brother's snarky comment.

While he hopes to avoid further scrutiny, Hayes recognizes this is an unlikely scenario as his brothers have never been ones to let things go. They are more of the harboring forever, will never let you forget it or live it down type.

Typical.

When his distraction efforts fail, Hayes excuses himself from the group and visits the bathroom. Throwing cold water on his face, he studies his reflection in the mirror, noticing a few more gray hairs today than even a few months back. He runs a hand over the stubble on his jaw, begging to be shaved, before retracing his steps to the living room.

"Did you just call your girlfriend?" Sam asks mockingly, playing along with the pick-on-Hayes game as he reenters the room.

Some things never change.

"Daddy!" Candace half-whines, catching on to the teasing taking place. "Does Uncle H really have a girlfriend?" Though she just turned six last week, Candace is perceptive for a kid and more outgoing than her sisters. She is high-energy like Wes but inquisitive like her mom, Lara—a perfect mix of the two.

"Oh, shut up," Hayes says, playfully punching Sam.

"Language, H," Wes scolds, with a raised brow in the direction of Candace, who is playing with her miniature kitchen set.

Shaking his head, Hayes sinks into the worn recliner without providing anyone the satisfaction of further acknowledgment.

Growing up, all three boys played sports together. Wes and Sam were always the more athletic ones, but what Hayes lacked in skill, he made up for with passion. Wes went on to play football at a local community college, a given considering his lineman build.

At the same time, Sam poured himself into baseball up until his junior year when a shoulder injury sent him to the bench. Unable to play anymore, Sam shifted his focus to healing and decided to pursue a career in medicine.

Though Hayes never quite understood their obsession with *playing* sports, he always enjoyed watching them, even to this day.

Since graduating from high school, though, Hayes hasn't spent much time at home or with his brothers aside from holidays and a once-in-a-blue-moon family vacation. Though his childhood was generally positive and happy, he was always ready to spread his wings and fly.

He had not looked back *until* his strong and fearless mother's health was threatened last year, taking an unexpected toll on everyone.

Now, Hayes spends at least three weekends a month playing caretaker, handling whatever it is his mom needs at the moment. And, because he can't resist her requests, most of these weekends also include quality time with his brothers—her dying wish to "be one big happy family again." *Who can say no to that?*

The forced togetherness was painful at first. Agonizing and dreadful, complete with awkward conversations and snappy comments. But now, almost a year into their new routine, Hayes enjoys his brothers' company and being called "Uncle H," even if it comes with some teasing every once in a while.

This afternoon, while their mom is resting from her most recent treatment, Hayes and the boys are enjoying a football marathon, arguing over who has the best fantasy team this season. While it is still too early to tell, Hayes is pleased with his team's performance, as evidenced by his trash talk and enthusiasm.

As the Bears' top receiver runs the length of the field, Hayes emerges from the pits of his recliner, whooping and hollering, appreciative of the extra points.

Fortunately, he survives the game, and the rest of the weekend, for that matter, unscathed. His to-do list is complete, and his mom is in good spirits. What more could he ask for?

Margaret.

As the weekend draws to a close, Hayes completes his goodbye ritual.

"It was good spending time with you, H," his mom says, her arms flung around his neck. "I worry about you being all alone and so far away."

Pulling away, Hayes takes in her petite frame and hollow features. "I know, Mama. But I'll be back before you know it. The boys will take care of you in the meantime."

Though she doesn't seem satisfied, she accepts the situation for what it is and steps out of her youngest son's way.

Hayes makes his way back to the airport, going through the motions on autopilot. The only thing out of the norm is *her* on his mind and, as a result, the warm and fuzzy feelings flurrying around inside.

Sitting at his gate and free from judgmental eyes, Hayes deems the coast clear to resume their conversation.

> **HAYES**
> *Looking forward to this evening… thinking we can meet at The Pearl at 6?*
>
> **MARGARET**
> *I'd love to, but the only thing is…*

She splits the message into two, causing his pulse to escalate, fearful of what she might say next.

> MARGARET
> *I don't go to dinner with people whose names I don't know...*

An audible laugh escapes his lips. He had completely forgotten she is likely still referring to him as "Mr. Americano." And while her message comes across as flirtatious banter, he senses it is rooted in truth.

They go back and forth briefly, and Hayes continues to play hard to get.

> HAYES
> *But you know my name, silly...*

> HAYES
> *It's Mr. Americano*

> MARGARET
> *Smooth! But no name, no date, mister.*

Is this a date?

Hayes shifts in his seat and clears his throat. Pressure builds in his chest.

A date? Did I call it a date? Did I give her the wrong impression?

Beads of sweat threaten to pill on his back at the thought of something so serious.

While Hayes has never been one for casual hookups, he's never been in the market for relationships, either.

"Love is a fragile gift," his mother used to remind him and his brothers growing up, often while looking at their dad with heart eyes. "It is so precious. Always take it seriously."

Ever since a car accident during his junior year took the life of his high school girlfriend, he has chosen to keep his distance, wary of commitment and fearful of heartbreak. Despite the idea of "the one" being intriguing, Hayes chooses to keep his guard up, doing all he can to avoid another loss.

He shakes the thought of old wounds and shifts his focus to what he might prepare for today's *hangout*, still refusing to call it a date.

> MARGARET
> *Anyway, you said you were traveling. Where to?*

Having successfully dodged her first inquiry *and* the date debacle, Hayes resolves to answer honestly.

> HAYES
> *Yep. Chicago. Just here for a few days. Nice to have a little weather change;)*
> *Did you do anything exciting this weekend?*

Hayes wishes he could unsend the message, wanting to save all his talking points for later. But, everyone knows despite it being September, cooler temps are nowhere in the forecast in Texas. He'd be lying if he said he didn't miss the cool Illinois breeze when down South.

> MARGARET
> *I'm jealous! I'm sure it's nice to get away and take your mind off things for a little bit. Mine was pretty low-key! Just relaxing.*

Surprisingly, she doesn't ask for more information, allowing him to fly under the radar for now.

Margaret attaches a photo of what he assumes to be an americano, the dark brown liquid challenging to identify through the phone. Studying the image, Hayes notices a little set of eyes peeking through the handle of the mug and begging for attention.

> HAYES
> *When can I meet your dog?*
>
> MARGARET
> *We'll see how tonight goes. Maybe you'll get lucky.*
>
> HAYES
> *Lucky? I hope so...*

His mind races, causing him to think about a hell of a lot more than meeting her dog.

> MARGARET
> *Don't get your hopes up. I have high expectations;)*
>
> HAYES
> *I'd expect nothing less.*
>
> MARGARET
> *What does that mean?*
>
> HAYES
> *It's a good thing. Relax.*

They text a bit longer, exchanging more flirtatious banter and metaphorical messages. Based on the natural flow and ease of conversation, Hayes assumes they will have a lot more in common than just their coffee orders. This realization makes him shift in his already tight middle seat, slightly uncomfortable and nervous at the thought of *more*.

As the plane picks up speed on the runway, he sends one last message to appease her before shutting off his phone.

>HAYES
>*Hayes.*

CHAPTER 6

Curled on the couch with Penelope Grace in her lap and *Grey's Anatomy* playing on the TV, Margaret is startled by the vibration of an incoming call.

The sight of *Mr. Americano/Hayes* running across her screen in a banner formation makes her go numb.

What the hell?

Chunking her phone in the air like a hot potato, Margaret has a mini freak-out moment before collecting herself, sitting up straight, and clicking *accept*.

"Hello?" she asks more as a question than a confident greeting, hating how her voice sounds.

Fidgeting and awaiting his response, Margaret stands and paces the length of the kitchen island in excited anticipation. Her nerves are in *full force*.

"Hey! Sorry if I caught you at a bad time!" he says with an uplifting tone, seemingly unfazed by her teenage girl jitters. "I just thought it would be easier to figure out our plans over the phone instead of text."

How mature.

Biting her lip and still pacing, Margaret slips her hair behind her ear and waits for him to continue. "I was thinking

I could be in charge of the food, and you can bring the drinks?" He pauses briefly, but just as she opens her mouth to agree, he adds, "I feel like you are a wine expert, so I'll leave that up to you."

Suppressing a sarcastic laugh and leaning against the counter to steady herself, Margaret says, "I wouldn't call myself an expert, but I'd be happy to grab some for us!"

"Wonderful. Is there anything, in particular, you'd like to eat?"

"Nope, I'm not picky," Margaret assures him.

For the most part, that's true. Of course, there are a few things that she absolutely despises, but she keeps them to herself, not wanting to come across as high maintenance on date one.

"Excellent." His voice sounds distant, as if his gears are already spinning. "I'll pull something together."

Trying to envision him at this moment and wondering what he's doing, Margaret hears what she thinks is a door closing behind him. She paints a picture in her mind of what his home might look like. *Masculine. Well-kept.*

Doing her best to disguise her racing heart, Margaret asks, "Can you drop me a pin or something for where I should meet you? I'm not super familiar with the area."

"Yep. Parking can kind of be a nightmare, so I'll meet you in my secret spot, then we can walk over."

"O-oh, okay. That works," Margaret manages, flustered by the words "secret spot" and the goosebumps they trigger.

Hanging up, she is struck by how natural their conversation seems. For a fleeting moment, she forgot that, previously, she had only said about twenty words to him, most of which were incoherent. Flashing back to their interaction at The

Brew, embarrassment washes over her again. *What was I thinking?*

Hanging up, Margaret glances at the clock. 4:27 p.m. Crunch time.

After pulling out every outfit in her closet, she settles on a casual, chic ensemble. While it is not too over-the-top or flashy, her old blue jean shorts and slouchy, off-the-shoulder blouse combo convey clear effort. And no outfit is complete without a dainty necklace and some pearl earrings.

Her room is now a disaster. Margaret throws hot rollers in for a soft yet voluminous curl to tame her Sunday afternoon nap hair. She then adds a delicate coating of blush and mascara to complete the look, knowing the little details make the biggest differences.

Fearful of being late, Margaret leaves close to an hour in advance, giving her plenty of time to assess the wine selection at the grocery store on her way. Out the door with a corkscrew in hand, Margaret has an uncontrollable pep in her step and a grin on her face.

Aware a person's wine selection says a lot about them, she is not ashamed to stand in the middle of the aisle, reading label after label, as if she were in a bookstore trying to find the perfect novel. Eventually, she settles on a bottle of prechilled chardonnay, aiming to satisfy his light and crisp expectations.

Margaret navigates toward the pin her handsome date provided, her chest tightening with anticipation as if she were approaching the peak of a roller coaster.

She does everything she can to calm her nerves, turning the AC on full blast and pulsing Shania Twain through the speakers for added confidence.

"Just be you. It's gonna be fine. Calm. Cool. Collected," she whispers.

Whipping into a shaded parking spot, Margaret is touching up her lipstick and humming the lyrics to another anthem when a shadow emerges in her peripheral.

Tap, tap, tap

Her body is involuntarily twitching from surprise, and the breath knocked out of her. Margaret looks up to see none other than Mr. Americano standing outside her window, grinning.

She clutches her chest dramatically and forces a smile. Reaching for the volume knob to turn down her pump-up music, she sneaks one last peek at herself before killing the engine. Gathering her belongings from the passenger seat, Margaret emerges from the car on wobbly legs, fearful of falling into him.

His presence is undeniable. He takes up much more space than she remembers in the best way possible. She admires his light blue jeans and collared shirt and inhales his masculine scent, reminiscent of the men's department of Dillard's. A smile gradually creeps its way onto her face. After scaling him from head to toe, her eyes finally find his.

Wrapping her up into a comfortable albeit unfamiliar side hug, Hayes whispers, "Good to see you, Margaret."

Despite her best efforts not to read into the casual embrace, Margaret can't help but think of it as something she wants to experience a million times over.

As he pulls away, putting space between them, the butterflies come swarming back. Margaret is reminded of how she felt about her first crush. Absolutely smitten.

"Thanks for meeting me. I hope you like this place. It's one of my favorites in the area," Hayes says, gesturing at the scenery.

His presence, combined with the beautiful, century-old architecture and peacefulness of the river, leaves Margaret nearly breathless.

"I-I can't believe I've never been here!" she stutters. *Maybe San Antonio isn't that bad after all...*

Retrieving what looks to be an insulated cooler from the back of his truck, Hayes leads the way down a narrow gravel path toward the river. Margaret follows, the path not wide enough for them to walk side by side. The foliage and vegetation surrounding them are luscious and green, like something from a botanical garden.

As they cross the river via a small pedestrian bridge, Margaret feels on top of the world and like a character in a romantic movie. The birds chirping above them and car horns honking in the distance bring her back to reality. Rounding the corner, she's surprised to see a large, open green space populated with people perched on picnic blankets with lavish spreads in front of them.

Hayes scans the area before ultimately picking a place in the corner for them to plop down.

"Is this okay with you?" he asks, set to fan out the plaid picnic blanket he packed.

In awe of his preparedness, Margaret nods, her lips frozen into a half smile.

"Perfect," Hayes says proudly, the oversized blanket perfectly sprawled out on the turf.

Margaret finds her way to the ground first, forcing *him* to make the call on how close together or far apart they should sit. The anxiety it evokes makes her wonder if she is really ready for the dating world.

Get a grip. You don't have to overthink everything!

As the September sun gives way to a cotton candy sky, Hayes unpacks an assortment of food, like Mary Poppins extracting goods from her mystery bag. Though still warm outside, a refreshing breeze blows through, hinting that fall is on its way. Live music and chatter from other picnickers fill the silence.

"I didn't even think about there being music out here," says Margaret, doing her best to make small talk and get the conversation flowing.

"Yeah." He removes a sheet of cling wrap to reveal a perfectly curated charcuterie board. "It's not like an organized thing, but different musicians just come out and play for donations. Sometimes it's just a guitar or just a violin, and other times there are full-on bands. Pretty neat!"

He is so in the know.

"That is so cool!" Seizing the opportunity to broach the topic of travel, she adds, "Kinda gives me New York vibes."

Hayes lights up at her mention of the Big Apple and proceeds to share memories and favorite spots from various trips. His excitement leaves Margaret seeing stars rather than a sunset.

Needing to look at something other than him for a moment, Margaret distracts herself by retrieving the bottle of wine she strategically selected. After impressing Hayes with her corkscrew skills, she gives each of the insulated glasses she packed a hefty pour.

Hayes initiates a toast to San Antonio and iced americanos, so Margaret hoists her glass in the air to meet his. With their eyes locked together, they each take their first sip of the Château Ste Michelle Chardonnay and smile bashfully.

"Wow, I'm impressed. Great pick!" he says, reaching for the bottle and studying the Columbia Valley wine's label.

"Why, thank you very much." Margaret attempts a faux bow, suppressing a sigh of relief. "I'm glad you like it!"

The truth is, she thought about branching out and trying something fancy but opted to go with this tried-and-true option because it's cheap and consistent. Happy with her decision, Margaret takes another swig.

"So, are you always a wine gal?" Hayes inquires, his head tilted slightly to the side.

"I'll drink just about anything but rum," Margaret admits, having been scarred by the spirit a few years back. "But I'd say wine is my go-to."

He studies her like he's trying to figure out his next move in a game of chess. "Are you more of a white or red person?"

"It depends. I like both," she admits. "I think I drink white more since it's so light and refreshing, but nothing beats a bold, tannic red paired with a rich pasta or steak." A subtle moan escapes her mouth at the thought.

Eyeing her and taking another sip, he says, "Look at you, throwing around the lingo."

His sarcasm and sense of humor make her blush. "Cliché, I know," she prefaces, not wanting to come across as *that* girl but knowing he will likely appreciate the story. "But I credit my limited knowledge to a trip I went on in college. It's crazy what six weeks in Italy will do to you," Margaret says, equal parts serious and sarcastic.

Stacking various accoutrements onto a cracker and popping them into his mouth, Hayes demands *more* details.

Margaret starts her spiel, the memories flooding back and sparking much joy. She talks about her roommate, their apartment near Santa Croce, the courses she took, and how she fell into a green pond. Margaret catches herself oversharing and speaking like an auctioneer, so she trails off apologetically.

"No, please continue. I want to hear it all," he assures her, his smile confirming he's unfazed by her rambles.

They discuss their jobs, families, and interests. Thanks to the wine and the discovery of so many similarities, their conversation flows easily, allowing Margaret's nerves to eventually subside.

"I travel a lot for my job. I don't hate it, though," Hayes says, swirling his glass and fiddling with a leaf that landed in his lap. "It's allowed me to see a lot of unique places, eat a lot of delicious food, meet a lot of interesting people…" His eyes land on Margaret.

Interesting people?

Margaret's nod and full mouth force him to continue.

"The last few years have been crazy, though." His legs outstretched, Hayes leans back, propping himself up with both hands. "I was living abroad when the pandemic started. Obviously, I had to come home, which was fine, but to go from London to my parents' house? Not so fine." He chuckles. "It's been good for us, but you could say my world was pretty much flipped upside down."

"Wow," is all she can manage.

"But, as you know, every job has pros and cons. I just try to pay more attention to the pros."

Margaret internalizes everything he is sharing, admiring his optimism and drive.

She keys in on one particular notion to probe deeper on. "You lived abroad? I'm so jealous! Where? For how long?" The questions and excitement spill out as she sits up, eager to hear more.

Bubbling with passion, Hayes shares his story with pride and enthusiasm. Though genuine and honest, at times, he sounds slightly rehearsed. "Well, there are a lot of answers to that. Most recently, I was in London, as I mentioned. Before that, I worked in Rome, Munich, and Paris. Surprisingly, Munich was a favorite of mine. When the world shut down, or whatever you want to call it, I had been consulting abroad for almost four years. I was in a really good place career-wise when it all went to shit," he confides with a somewhat bitter laugh.

Four years? Wow. How old is this guy?

All this time, Margaret had assumed Hayes was close to her age, but his extensive background and work history gave her pause.

"Wow! That's amazing!" she says, searching for the best, least obtrusive way to ask his age. She does some quick calculations to figure out when he most likely graduated from college, but struggling to think clearly, she opts to just ask instead. "So, when did you graduate then? And did you go right into consulting?"

"About eight years ago," he says, twisting the class ring on his right hand. "As much as it pains me to say, I'll be thirty next year." He fakes a pained expression and takes a sip.

"Just think of yourself as a fine wine—only getting better with age," Margaret says, winking. "Not to mention wiser and more mature, too, I'm sure."

Her timely joke a hit, as evidenced by his smile and belly laugh, Margaret navigates back to their previous topic.

"Anyway, what was your favorite part about living abroad?" Margaret asks with a slightly raised and inquisitive eyebrow.

"Oh, there are so many things," Hayes says, running his hand through his hair and looking off into the distance. "Honestly? The food." He pauses as if unsure about the explanation he wants to give. "I think it's so cool how a country's food reflects the culture and the people. Like in France, everything is centered around meals, family, and being together." His tone softens as he appears to reflect. "I tried to learn as much as I could while I was there... Maybe I can teach you a thing or two sometime," he adds, giving her shoulder a playful nudge.

Their conversation flows from their love of good food and drinks to other topics of shared interest like live music, cooking, attending sporting events, the beach, and family.

Little by little, Hayes reveals nuggets about himself. He speaks highly of his parents and sounds proud of his siblings, all of whom he has spent a lot more time with recently.

Pleased with all that she is hearing, Margaret tries to memorize as many tidbits as she can for both her friends and her journal entry later on.

The sun has set, and the moon has claimed its space. All the while, his eyes remain fixated on her. Cooling temperatures and the occasional yawn cause Margaret to steal a glance at her phone.

"When did it get so late? I completely lost track of time!" she says, shocked to discover almost four hours have passed.

Glancing up at the night sky, Hayes says, "Well, time flies when you're having fun."

Margaret catches herself anticipating his half smile and is hit with a feeling she can't shake.

I want to get to know him so well that I can predict everything he does.

"That it does," she agrees, finishing the only swig left in her glass.

Gathering their things and mindlessly cleaning up the area, the idea of "what's next" looms in the air.

Hayes breaks the silence. "So…" He pauses. "I was thinking we could do this again, or something else sometime? That is, if you're interested and have another free night."

If I have a free night? I want to laugh at that statement. Only every night.

"I'd love that!" she exclaims, with a tad more enthusiasm than intended.

Approaching their cars, Margaret drops her things into the backseat before turning to find Hayes standing unusually close. Without missing a beat, he gently grabs her chin with his thumb and index finger, bringing their lips together as if he has done it a million times before.

Margaret can't help but notice how well they fit together like two long-lost puzzle pieces.

Savoring the moment, she refrains from pulling away.

When they eventually split, she allows her gaze to linger on him, alternating between his eyes and his lips, attempting to memorize both.

"I couldn't help myself," Hayes admits unapologetically. He releases his grip on her waist. "I've wanted to do that since we got here." His low volume and raspy voice almost make her knees buckle.

Margaret simply nods in affirmation, willing her patience and silence to extract more raw emotion and honesty.

"Actually, if I'm being completely honest, I've wanted to do that since I saw you at The Brew."

Her heart threatening to beat out of her chest, Margaret rises on her tiptoes, allowing their lips to collide again. "Me too," she manages, almost breathless.

CHAPTER 7

Margaret is hardly out of the parking lot before her phone lights up with an incoming message from the one and only.

> MR. AMERICANO/HAYES
> *I had a great time tonight. Let's do it again soon?*

Her lips were tingling, her head was spinning, and her heart was racing. Margaret was eager to update her college besties on Mr. Americano. Far removed from the I-might-have-just-met-the-one phase of life, she's sure they will want all the details regarding her date with the eye candy from the coffee shop.

Prepared to share everything about her fairytale evening, Margaret discovers the group chat is already buzzing with chatter about Caroline's bachelorette party this weekend, planned by her over-the-top sister and maid of honor, Reagan.

> TESS
> *What am I supposed to pack again? I haven't been thinking about anything besides how excited I am to see all of you!*

> SUSANNAH
> IDK I'm prioritizing comfort and avoiding anything tight. I'm in that awkward is-she-pregnant-or-is-she-not phase.... :/

> CAROLINE
> I have it easy this time! I'm dumping everything white I own into a suitcase and calling it done!

Caroline attaches a color-coded itinerary detailing the celebration from arrival to lingerie shower, karaoke, and spa experience, with a photo-op highlighted at every point. *Great.*

Still behind the wheel, Margaret can only glance at the unnecessarily detailed document, but even that is enough to earn an eye roll and her phone a free trip to the passenger seat.

I cannot think about that right now.

Long after she makes it home and tends to PG, her cheeks still twitch from smiling so hard.

Despite their best efforts, Margaret and Hayes find it challenging to settle on a date and time right away due to their work schedules and other commitments.

> MARGARET
> We can play it by ear if we need to. Maybe same time next week?

> MR. AMERICANO/HAYES
> That works for me. I was just hoping to see you again before then...

MARGARET
What's that old saying? Distance makes the heart grow fonder?;)

Though bummed, she would be lying if she said this doesn't compound her excitement.

He emphasizes her last message. Margaret snaps a quick screenshot for the archives, knowing the girls will *love* this.

Against her will, Margaret engages in the anticipatory weekend exchanges, plotting her "retro cowgirl" costume for karaoke night and agreeing to sing one song with Caroline, but only if it's Carrie Underwood.

In addition to how excited they are for Caroline's bachelorette party extravaganza, the quad manages to cover everything from dinner recipe inspiration to new dry shampoo recommendations and what they are currently watching on Netflix in less than an hour and a half.

They transition from topic to topic without any kind of segue as a result of the language they've developed over the years. The fact that it makes no sense to outsiders doesn't faze them one bit.

I love that about us.

However, the right time never presents itself for Margaret to mention her new beau. Content with keeping him to herself *and* dodging their questions, she decides to hold off a little longer.

Their fun and lighthearted conversation—combined with the reality of all being under the same roof again in less than five days—sent her to bed with a hopeful smile.

* * *

When the weekend finally arrives, Margaret pledges to have a good attitude, despite how frilly and "Instagram-worthy" all of it is. She enters the cottage-style Airbnb in downtown Austin with her bag full of preplanned and color-coordinated outfits, lingerie gifts, and four bottles of wine—Château Ste Michelle Chardonnay, of course, her contribution to the weekend's bar cart.

Her friends greet her at the door with a group hug, causing all of Margaret's feelings of annoyance and subconscious jealousy to dissipate.

"Hi, ladies!" she says, her voice muffled by the commotion.

"Finally! Reunited at last!" Caroline cheers gleefully, spinning around and showing off her first *of many* all-white ensembles.

With ease, they fall back into their old ways of finishing each other's sentences, laughing until they cry, and incorporating as many inside jokes as possible. Similar to riding a bike, it never takes long for them to get back into the swing of things.

The tone shifts slightly as other bridal party members arrive, including coworkers, cousins, and childhood friends. Margaret is one of three people in the group without a ring on her left hand. Though she pretends not to notice, the truth is, it makes her anxious and slightly embarrassed.

After a full night of dancing, singing, laughing, and chatting, the girls catch a few hours of sleep in preparation for day two. Wearing various shades of pink, they depart for brunch and bottomless mimosas, followed by endless shopping and pampering.

Though the group attempts to mix and mingle, Margaret tends to stay close to Caroline, Tess, and Susannah. By midafternoon, her face and abs ache from the constant laughing.

"I've missed you guys so much," Margaret says, longing for simpler times as they walk down the sidewalk like a brick wall, their arms intertwined and feet in lockstep.

"Me too. We need more girl weekends," Caroline decides.

"We'll all be together again before you know it for the *actual* big day!" Susannah says.

The wedding. Just what I need.

Margaret hates herself for the spiteful thought, knowing they have all dreamed of sharing this special day for years.

Her pity is interrupted when Tess says, "I think it would be fun if we planned a trip for just the four of us sometime soon. Where there aren't a million distractions or other people," she mumbles, not wanting to offend anyone else in the bridal party that's not in their clique.

Still walking to their next activity, a brewery east of downtown, they brainstorm logistics—when, where, and how. Unsurprisingly, spouses, impending motherhood, jobs, and preexisting plans give them pause. It feels nearly impossible to come up with even a halfway viable plan.

Margaret doesn't allow disappointment to take over. Instead, she remains positive and has a blast celebrating the newest name change of the group. Her fringe and floral outfit, accessorized with a pink cowboy hat, complemented her single karaoke performance beautifully, *and* she earned a standing ovation from the crowd. Success.

The group doesn't make it back to their home base until after midnight. Buzzing from the wine and cocktails they consumed at dinner, Reagan had the bright idea to order pizza.

Her best idea yet.

After changing into their matching pajamas and scarfing down copious amounts of carbs, a contagion of yawns ripples through the group, signaling the end of another successful day. And knowing tomorrow's schedule begins bright and early with sunrise yoga, no one argues.

Seriously, whose idea was sunrise yoga? Oh, yeah. Reagan.

"I can't bounce back like I used to," Tess admits.

"Ugh, me either, sister," says the bride-to-be. "I'm gonna need to bust out some eye patches in the morning, or else I'll look like a raccoon in all of our pictures!"

"Things we say now," Margaret says, shaking her head and acknowledging that she sounds just like her mother.

Fortunately, the party doesn't have to end quite yet. Caroline staked a claim on the only double queen room in the house on their behalf, so Margaret and her pals continued to catch up and reminisce just like in the old days.

When the room finally falls silent, Margaret summons the courage to speak up and share her news. Her eyes fixated on the texturized wallpaper, illuminated by the light of a streetlamp peeking in through the window, Margaret declares, "I have a confession."

Lying next to her, Tess springs upright to a ninety-degree angle. *"Spill!"*

"Well," Margaret begins, dragging out the word for emphasis, wishing she would have thought through her saga more intentionally. "I met some—"

"You what? And you're just now telling us?" Susannah rushes to her bedside to interrogate without allowing Margaret to so much as finish the sentence.

The girls begin peppering questions her way, leaving no time for her to *actually* answer them.

As expected.

It doesn't take long for them to catch on to her game and chill out enough for her to respond. Like middle schoolers at a sleepover, the girls cram into one bed altogether for story time. Margaret, Tess, and Caroline sit in various crouched positions, hugging their knees, while Susannah is sprawled out, combating back pain.

Margaret folds her hands in her lap and waits with a sly smile plastered on her face, pretending to be bashful.

"Well," she begins again, this time with actual intent to continue. "We met at The Brew, my new favorite coffee shop, a few weeks ago. There was a little mix-up with our orders, and somehow, I ended up with his number as a result!" She flicks her hair over her shoulder for added emphasis.

Oohs and ahhs come from her audience, giving Margaret flashbacks to when she told the same story to Britt.

"We've texted a little bit and been on one date. So far, we've really hit it off. It seems like we have a lot in common!" Her tone lifts at the end, a reflection of her optimism and persuasiveness peeking through, her desire to sell them on the idea of Mr. Americano prevalent.

"Do you think he's the one?" Tess asks with wiggling eyebrows and a big grin, always taking things to the extreme.

"What's his name? What do you know about him? Do you have any mutual friends?" Susannah asks as the metaphoric and soon-to-be literal mom of the group. Margaret can tell, based on her mischievous look, Susannah is already wanting to do some sleuthing and run a background check.

"What does he look like? Show us a pic!" says Caroline, often the one to care about people's *outward* appearances first.

Margaret does her best to answer their questions honestly and without giving away too much. She elaborates on their date from last weekend, her eagerness for the next becoming more and more apparent with every word.

"It was literally so perfect. He planned it all, from the place to the picnic to the conversation topics and everything in between." Feeling a little sales-y and having flashbacks to a class she took on influence in college, Margaret dials it back a notch. "It was never weird or awkward or anything."

Though the room is dark, Margaret can still see the darting eyes all around her, magnified by the deafening silence.

"So, did you say you do have mutual friends or not?" Tess asks, circling back.

Resolving to maintain her transparency, Margaret says, "Um, honestly? I'm not sure yet."

This raises some eyebrows, but Margaret remains steadfast and unwavering. "We just haven't gotten to that yet."

"Where does he live?" Caroline asks, familiar with the San Antonio area and its various neighborhoods.

Fearful of how they might respond if she admits another unknown, Margaret opts to stretch the truth a bit. "Near the river, I think." Presumably, this *is* true based on The Brew and Hayes's recommendation of The Pearl, but she makes a mental note to confirm.

Giggling and offering a side eye, Caroline says, "Silly, the river practically goes all the way to the Coast! That could mean anything!"

Touché.

Margaret shrugs and remains quiet, not wanting to dig a deeper hole for herself.

As the interrogation continues, Margaret's self-consciousness increases. Their doubt and hesitation put a real damper on her mood, causing her posture and tone to weaken. Her vivacious storytelling and giddiness are replaced with skepticism and sadness.

The clock now reads 2:54 a.m. Looking for a way to escape, Margaret fakes a few yawns and promises to share more in the morning.

Caroline and Susannah return to their bed as Tess and Margaret resituate on their own.

That wasn't the way it was supposed to go.

Lying on her side, directly facing the wall, Margaret can't shake the feeling that they aren't on her side at all.

Like they don't *think* it will work.

Like they don't *want* it to work.

Having been the seventh wheel for the majority of their friendship, this realization causes tears to prick the backs of her eyelids. Instead of being happy for her, they jumped to conclusions, offering "watch-outs" rather than encouragement.

Margaret struggles to fall asleep with her mind and heart at war with one another. She replays both her date with Hayes and her conversation with her friends, trying to decipher the details and nuances of each.

He's been nothing but kind and a gentleman thus far. Why can't they just be happy for me? Could they be right? But what if he is the one?

CHAPTER 8

―――

Walking into his temporary, company-issued rental home, Hayes flips on the light switch and drops his duffle bag to the floor. Surveying the unfinished place, he does some mental math to calculate how much longer he will be in this hell hole.

When he initially transitioned to this San Antonio project almost a year ago, it was supposed to be temporary. "It's a turnkey project," his boss had promised. "You'll be in and out and on to the next thing in no time."

A standard three-month turnaround? Bullshit.

Around the six-month marker, he was at his wit's end and tired of packing all his belongings up every single weekend to vacate his small, sterile hotel room. Fortunately, he was able to negotiate alternative housing accommodations in the form of a monthly stipend.

Hayes has tried to make the most of the unusual situation. He came across this place on Zillow, and though dilapidated, it meets his needs and allows him to save a little money for when the time for a *real house* comes. Still spending a good portion of his time traveling, he was really only looking for a place to cook, sleep, and shower. This suffices.

The vibration in his pocket brings him out of his pity party.

> MARGARET
> Are we still on for tonight? *fingers crossed*

> HAYES
> You bet we are! Anything, in particular, you want to do?

> MARGARET
> I don't really have any ideas... I'm flexible!

Sitting on his only piece of living room furniture, an outdoor beanbag he bought from Target's end-of-summer season sale, Hayes has a lightbulb moment.

> HAYES
> Do you like sushi?

> MARGARET
> Love it! What kind of crazy person doesn't?

> HAYES
> You'd be surprised... I'm glad you passed the test.

Hayes smiles childishly, her humor putting him in better spirits.

> HAYES
> I have a plan;)

Between texts, Hayes cleans up, rinsing off the airport filth and preparing for his casual date night plans. His idea for the evening is a little DIY sushi session at home. The only problem being Hayes doesn't consider this place to be "home." It is an embarrassing dump.

> MARGARET
> What do you have in mind?

Her question makes him pause. Leaning against the bathroom counter, he considers his options. Wanting to maintain the surprise and anticipation, he opts for only inquiring about the essentials.

> HAYES
> Well... what would you think about me bringing stuff over to your place? Is that okay with you?

Tension pools inside him as he anxiously awaits her response.
   I hope she says yes and doesn't think I'm some sort of creep.

> MARGARET
> Um sure?

> HAYES
> Fantastic. Thank you! If you'll flip me your address and what time I should be there, I'll take care of everything else.

Once she provides both, he goes about his business, acquiring everything they'll need for the evening and a few extra treats for good measure. With her address plugged into his phone, he makes the twelve-minute drive across town to her apartment.

Hayes knocks at her front door, his arms full of sushi-making materials and stomach swirling with nerves. On one hand, it feels like they haven't seen each other in forever, but on the other hand, it feels like just yesterday, he was pulling her in for their first kiss. And because the moment feels so normal, he practically forgets this is only *hangout* number two.

Still not a date.

"Hey!" Margaret cheers, flinging the door open.

"I come bearing gifts," he says, gesturing to the grocery bags in both of his hands. "Prepare to sushi."

"Amazing. Come on in, and make yourself at home," she calls over her shoulder. "Penelope, say hi to our guest. And stay out of the way," she instructs the little dog attacking his ankles.

Following her lead through the elongated apartment to her kitchen, Hayes walks slowly, admiring the decor and avoiding the excited canine romping around.

"It's so nice to meet the famous Penelope Grace. It's a pleasure to be in your presence," Hayes teases, setting down the food before bending to rub her belly.

Flouncing like a fish out of water, Penelope is beyond ecstatic about the attention she's receiving. *Mission accomplished.*

Beaming with pride, Margaret announces, "Don't take it lightly. I don't introduce her to just anyone. She's my roommate, child, therapist… She has a lot of responsibilities. It just depends on the day."

"Understandable," Hayes says, slowly spinning in a circle and taking in his surroundings.

The place is colorful and meticulously clean, neither of which surprises him. Photos and various pieces of art cover the walls as a calming playlist fills the air and a vanilla candle burns on the coffee table. It looks, feels, and smells comfortable.

Homey. Like her.

"So, what do we have here?" Margaret asks, pulling items out of the paper grocery bags one by one. "Wine? Off to a good start."

"Want me to get it opened up?"

"That'd be great!" Margaret says graciously, extending the bottle and an accompanying opener to him before continuing through the contents.

Pulling the items out individually, she creates a spread on the counter of their materials. Everything from a salmon filet to imitation crab to fresh vegetables, various sauce bottles, seaweed wraps, and a box of rice.

Her eyes wide and scanning the setup, Margaret says, "Wow. I'm not sure what I've signed myself up for…"

"Don't freak-out. It's gonna be fun," he assures her, his hands placed on her shoulders. "It takes a little time upfront, then we get to enjoy it," he says, handing her a glass of refreshing white wine as a distraction.

Her skeptical look and piercing brown eyes give him pause and send flurries down his spine.

"Okay. I can do this," she says, taking a sip. "What's first?"

Hayes spells out the to-do list, beginning with rice cooking and ingredient prep. "The rice takes the longest, so we'll want to get that going. Then it's just a lot of chopping pretty much."

"I can manage that. I make a great sous-chef." She flicks her hair over her shoulder for dramatic effect as her eyes trail over his body.

They busy themselves in the kitchen, continuing to laugh and joke through the onion-induced tears, Penelope interruptions, and spilled sauce mishaps. With the rice cooked and cooled, they prepare for the next step.

"Okay, now for the fun part!" Hayes cheers, standing close behind her, taking in the coconut scent of her shampoo. "Let's get rolling!"

"I need help from the expert," Margaret faux whines, batting her eyelashes at him.

"Your wish is my command." Using her plea for help as an excuse, he inches closer to her, his front grazing up against her back, both of their hearts beating audibly. He wraps his arms around her, setting up her workstation and guiding her hands through the process.

Their breathing is uneven, and their hands are growing shaky. Margaret sets down the rice spoon and pushes the mat away. Hayes, tensing up, swallows the lump in his throat as she turns, now closer than before, and looks up at him expectantly.

"Sorry, I can't focus on that," she apologizes, her voice quiet and faint.

Her eyes are searching his face. Hayes suppresses his thoughts of doubt, grabs her face in his hands, and presses his body against hers, relying on the sushi-cluttered countertop for balance.

They linger, molded together, for what feels like forever. He runs his hands along her body, accentuating every curve and judging each reaction. When they finally separate, their puckered lips are replaced with sweet smiles.

"I've thought about that every day for the last week." Hayes takes a step back and chuckles. "You are something else."

Halfway covering her rosy cheeks with her hands, she agrees. "Me too. I knew the sushi could wait, but I couldn't."

For the rest of the evening, they split their attention between each other's lips and their sushi. They talk, laugh, and tease each other, alternating between playful sarcasm and raw honesty.

By the time they call it a night, Hayes can think of nothing else but doing it all over again.

And again. And again.

* * *

Normally, Hayes's days are long, frustrating, and stressful. But today, despite the typical management issues, budgeting decisions, and impending timelines, time flew by. Perhaps it had something to do with the fact that he couldn't stop thinking about Margaret's laugh, running his fingers through her hair and his lips colliding with hers. Happy distractions.

After a few beers and some Chinese takeout from his favorite hole-in-the-wall restaurant down the street, Hayes bites the bullet and sends a damn text. Enough with the overthinking bullshit.

So what if she hasn't texted me today?

Instead of formulating twenty-two versions of a text and going with option number one, Hayes opts for an off-the-cuff message that he hopes will catch her attention.

> HAYES
> *Is there anything better than a beer to celebrate the end of a Monday? Cheers*

He clicks *send*, attaching an image of his half-empty Coors for good measure. So that she knows he's being serious.

Sitting in his trusty bean bag, watching an old rerun of *Dateline* and attempting to tune out the sirens wailing in the distance, he is thrilled when his phone dings.

Was she thinking about me too?

> MARGARET
> *Yes... not drinking *alone* on a Monday hehe*

She, too, attaches photographic evidence.

Hayes decides to continue down the straightforward, no-bullshit, say-what-you-feel path tonight because why not? It's a valid question. If the last year has taught him anything, it is to cut to the chase. No need to beat around the bush. Life is too short for games.

> HAYES
> *Touché. Why are we drinking alone?*

> MARGARET
> *Great question. I don't know. How about let's not drink alone tomorrow?*

The *Dateline* crime is almost solved, and the sun has officially set. Hayes catches his heart beating faster than before. Though they've only been on two dates so far, he aches for her to be close. Her infectious joy and bubbly attitude put him at ease like nothing else he's experienced.

> HAYES
> Fred's?

> MARGARET
> You read my mind

> HAYES
> Great minds think alike!

> MARGARET
> I'm flattered you think I have a great mind;)

> HAYES
> I think you have more than a great mind

He presses send without giving it a second thought. But when he doesn't get another immediate response, he follows up for added clarity.

> HAYES
> …. like a great personality, sense of humor, coffee preferences, smile, hair, etc.

Still nothing.

Maybe completely honest and unfiltered isn't the way to go.

Rubbing his temples and regretting his approach, he wonders what might be circling through her head right now. Did he just ruin any chance he had, or, by some miracle, did he seal the deal?

CHAPTER 9

Thump. Thump. Thump.

Margaret's heart threatens to beat out of her chest. Lacking confidence in her flirting skills, she drops her phone and propels herself into the pile of plush pillows on her bed. She lays face down and pounds the comforter with her fist.

"Ahh!" she fake screams into the fluff. *You're fine. Just tell him you like him back.*

> MARGARET
> *Why thank you. I think you're pretty great too, Mr. Americano;)*

Pressing *send*, she rolls over, now staring at her nightstand sprinkled with photos of her friends. The sight of them stirs up a mixture of emotions. From this weekend, their past, her future, and everything in between.

Their hesitancy about her new romantic interest hit her like a blow to the back, unexpected and disheartening. The conflict makes her stomach churn with anxiety, so she resumes her face down, head-in-the-pillows position because what *else* is she going to do?

She falls asleep in this spot, only to wake to her alarm with an aching neck and messy hair.

Tuesdays, per usual, are spent in the office, following Amanda from meeting to meeting and scribbling down notes along the way. Because of the mom guilt that comes with leaving Penelope Grace alone, Margaret resolves to bring her along for tonight's outing at Fred's.

"You have to be on your best behavior," she says. "That means no barking. Absolutely none."

Penelope looks at her, the whites of her eyes showing sarcastically as if to say, "Yeah, right. Whatever."

They make it to Fred's slightly ahead of schedule to claim their table. Penelope, wanting to play and wrestle with the dogs across the patio, pulls Margaret along. As they weave in and out of picnic tables and dodge servers, balancing trays of beer and bar bites, Margaret evaluates their table options. She eventually settles on a small two-top table near the river, where she ties Penelope up to avoid losing her in the crowd and fires Hayes a text.

> MARGARET
> *Grabbed a table in the back corner near the dog park. First round is on me. What's your drink of choice?*
>
> MR. AMERICANO/HAYES
> *Best message I've read all day*

His text makes her blush, per usual. Wiggling in her seat, she glances up nonchalantly to ensure no one is watching her, sitting alone and smiling at her phone because *how embarrassing.*

MR. AMERICANO/HAYES
Beer. Surprise me.

MARGARET
The pressure! Never fear. I can handle it.

A beat later, their waiter for the evening approaches, giving Margaret only a split second to make a decision. He waits patiently, then scribbles Margaret's request for a Coors Light and a Fred's Frosé before heading to the next table.

Thinking about Britt and the many frosés they shared, she pulls up their messages to check-in. Knowing their schedules are generally opposite, she tries not to get her hopes up but decides to initiate anyway.

Not long after, Hayes and their drinks arrive in unison. Margaret emerges from her stool only to be engulfed by his arms in a bear hug. "Hi!" she giggles, her head pressed into his neck. "Hope I met your beer expectations."

Grinning, he peeks over her shoulder at the silver can awaiting his attention. "Exceeded."

Pretending to wipe sweat from her brow, Margaret says, "Whew! I was worried!"

They wiggle in their barstools, unsteady on the gravel ground, and lock eyes for their first sip.

Unsure where to begin, Margaret inquires about his workday and comments on his attire. "You sure are looking sharp," she says as he loosens his shirt, revealing a few more inches of his chest. "You look good in blue."

"I wish I had a dollar for every time my mom told me that growing up," he says sarcastically. Then, in air quotes and a mocking tone, "'It makes your eyes pop!'"

Margaret snickers, imagining the scene unfold. "I can just picture it. She's right!"

She takes the opportunity to inquire more about his parents and childhood. Learning about his brothers and their families, Margaret makes a note to report back to her skeptic friends.

"Enough about me," he says. "I want to know more about you!"

Inspired by his vulnerability and willingness to share about his family, Margaret does the same, divulging more than she did on their first two dates. She shares what it was like growing up in Conrad, a place where everybody knows everybody. "At the time, I couldn't wait to get out," she reflects, her gaze fixated on the table's wood grain. "But now, I realize it wasn't all that bad of a place to grow up. And I wouldn't be totally opposed to moving back one day."

Margaret takes a sip of her drink, surprised to have just admitted that to herself, much less said it out loud.

"Sounds like a pretty great place! And not all that different from where I grew up."

They toss around stories of their youth as if they are walking down memory lane hand in hand.

For a minute, they sit in silence, admiring the sunset reflecting on the river nearby. Penelope Grace, posed and poised at Margaret's feet, recuperates before engaging with other furry friends.

It is Hayes who breaks the stillness by saying, "Let's play twenty questions."

"I don't know the last time I played that. We alternate asking the questions, right?" she asks.

"Yes, but we both have to answer all of the questions. It's only fair," Hayes adds, shooting her a wink as he drinks his beer.

Margaret nods. "Deal. You go first."

They exchange questions effortlessly, starting with familiar topics they have broached in other conversations before digging deeper. They cover everything from college majors to dream jobs, irrational fears, and dream home aesthetics, revealing just how well they balance each other out.

"Last question. This is serious," he says.

"I'm feeling pressured again," Margaret teases. She pauses, pretending to be deep in thought despite knowing full well what she is going to ask. Her fingers resting on her chin in a pondering position, she finally says, "What has been the best part of your day so far?"

Without hesitating and while looking her dead in the eyes, he says, "This."

Not expecting him to be so forthright, Margaret readjusts in her seat, hoping it will help her get a handle on the emotions swirling inside.

"I agree. The weather is perfect, and this place is so fun. Plus, the company isn't too bad either," Margaret says, reaching her hand across the small table to graze his.

Their fingers interlock, and Hayes gives hers a subtle squeeze that sends electricity through her veins.

During their time at Fred's, many stop by the table to pet PG, claiming she is "so adorable" and "totally irresistible." While their table guests have eyes on the dog, Margaret only has eyes for Hayes. And based on his continued physical touch and flirtatious comments, she presumes the feelings are reciprocated.

While Penelope has, in fact, been on her best behavior all evening, her sassiness begins to show when a cavapoo joins the table next to them. With Penelope unable to keep it together, Margaret resolves to call it a night.

They stroll to the parking lot, occasionally brushing their arms and intentionally drawing out their last few moments together.

Approaching their cars, Hayes takes her hand in his as he says, "I had fun tonight."

Looking up to her left, Margaret is struck by how handsome he is when backlit by the parking lot floodlights. A fluttering feeling fills her stomach, taking her longer than normal to string together a coherent sentence.

"Me too," she says softly. "I enjoy talking to you."

Slowing to a stop, Hayes positions himself directly in front of her and peers down. His eyes are so intently locked on her that it feels like he's staring holes into her soul.

Right as she makes a move to look away and catch her breath, his hands find their way to her cheeks and his lips to hers. Though she's been anticipating it all night, the embrace still catches her off guard.

They remain oblivious to the world until interrupted by a honking truck full of teenage boys. The pair takes the disturbance as their cue to part ways. Slowly pulling apart, their fingers linger in midair, a slow and dramatic split.

Slipping into her car, Margaret reaches for her phone to give Tess a call while the feelings are still fresh and lively inside.

"Hey, girl! How's it going?" Margaret asks, missing their casual impromptu check-ins.

"No complaints here! I just got off work a little bit ago. Headed home now. Where are you off to?" Tess asks.

Hesitant to share out of fear of what Tess might say, Margaret takes a deep breath and says, "Well, I'm actually headed home from happy hour with Hayes."

"OMG, tell me everything!" says Tess, her energy over-the-top despite her extra-long workday.

Margaret doesn't identify a single trace of reluctance or doubt in her friend's voice, and it's a pleasant surprise considering how last weekend went.

Margaret gives her the rundown, doing her best to communicate how easily Hayes checks every box. She shares what they ate and drank and a synopsis of the question game but chooses to leave out the details of their goodbye. Tess, snickering on the other end of the line, seems to be pleased with what she's hearing though undoubtedly wanting more steam and fewer boring facts.

"I'm so glad you had fun! He sounds pretty great. I can't wait to meet him and judge for myself," Tess says, attempting to sound as calm, collected, and supportive as possible. "But, you know I have to ask… did he kiss you again?" She draws out the last syllable for dramatic effect and emphasis, implying this kiss would mean more than the others. Tess has always read into every little thing—playing games, taking notes, and interpreting things Margaret has never thought twice about.

Because it was the best kiss of her life, and she is still buzzing from head to toe, Margaret concedes. Struggling to adequately describe their interaction in the dimly lit, almost deserted lot, Margaret accidentally lets a subtle, subconscious moan escape her mouth.

"OMG!" Tess repeats, this time even more stunned. "So, it wasn't *just* a kiss…"

Knowing Tess is most likely squirming around on the other end of the line, Margaret continues to appease her, selfishly wanting to relive the moment for herself.

"It felt so raw and meaningful. I guess because of the conversation we'd just had, we both felt really vulnerable and connected. I don't even know how long it lasted. I do know the only reason we stopped was that some dumbasses honked at us. It was literally so embarrassing!"

Tess laughs. "I remember those days. Granted, it's been like ten years, but I've been caught in a parking lot once or twice."

"Oh, geez, I can only imagine," Margaret says, trying to suppress the image of high school Tess making out with her now husband, Ben. "I don't need the details."

With a puff, Tess returns to asking logistical questions. "Did you find out where he lives? More about his family? You know I'm a sucker for a family man."

"No, I didn't ask for his address. Believe it or not, I'm trying *not* to come off as a crazy bitch," Margaret says with a slightly snarky tone. "And yes. Two brothers. Sam and Wes. Both older. Both married. They don't live around here. I know he's an uncle, but I can't recall all the details there. He spoke highly of his parents, which you know I always look for."

She rattles off detail after detail, hoping to make it out of the conversation unscathed.

"Yes, yes, all good things. When are you seeing him again? And more importantly, when can I meet him?"

"I don't know for sure, but soon." Margaret lets her response linger for Tess to process.

"You didn't answer both questions?" Tess asks, confused. "What about the weekend of the wedding? Is he coming? You should totally invite him!"

"No, he's not coming to Caroline's wedding. That sounds like a disaster waiting to happen. But we'll see," she answers hesitantly. "I can ask him if he's available to see if we can coordinate something, but no promises."

Margaret processes her friend's request.

It could work. But is he ready for that? Are we ready for that?

Exhaling, Margaret says, "Well, I just pulled up to the apartment. I'm gonna get Penelope situated and call it a night. Hope you're able to get some good rest!"

"Right back at ya! Thanks for calling. So good to hear your voice!" Tess says. "And I'm thrilled you had a good date, truly."

"Me too, thank you." Margaret agrees before pushing the red button.

As part of her new daily ritual, before setting her alarms and turning off the lights, Margaret completes her entry with a blushing smile plastered across her face.

The most perfect date. Asked & answered lots of questions, laughed a lot, and had the best kiss of my life. Didn't want it to end. Can't wait to do it again. He's amazing <3

CHAPTER 10

Back at The Brew, Hayes should be focused on preparing for next week's client pitch and his upcoming performance evaluation, but his mind is on other things… like the sound of Margaret's voice when she's telling a story that's important to her, the thrill of holding her hand as they walk along the riverside, and what it would be like to introduce her to his family.

Looking around, Hayes admires the bustling coffee shop with a line out the door of people, from high schoolers to retirees, all waiting for their coffee. His eyes land on Margaret sitting across from him, and he's struck with the reality that it has been almost two months since they bumped into each other here.

It feels like that was yesterday and a lifetime ago.

It only took a few weeks for Hayes and Margaret to establish a routine. Sunday evening picnics, typically at The Pearl, Happy Hour on Tuesdays, and the occasional midafternoon coffeeshop date here, at The Brew, where they work in silence alongside one another.

Margaret has extended a few invites to other social gatherings, none of which he has been able to attend. The clock is ticking until he is forced to come clean because he's running low on excuses. While Margaret has never pressed him for more details, he has grown to recognize the hesitant facial expression she makes when something isn't quite adding up.

His gaze on her rather than his computer screen, Hayes observes her biting her bottom lip and repositioning her hair, two habits he has grown to love.

He taps his pen along the table, attempting to parse his personal and professional thoughts apart.

How did I get in so deep so quickly?

Just as the thought crosses his mind, she pipes up. "What do you think about going to Fred's for live music and drinks tonight? I heard there's going to be an awesome cover band!"

"I wish I could. Maybe we can plan for next week?"

Her excited and irresistible smile immediately falls, activating a twinge of guilt in his gut. "Yeah, maybe," she says.

Hayes senses sadness more than skepticism, unsure which is worse.

But truly, if his mom didn't *need* him, things might be different. He might get to hang around and meet Margaret's friends, participate in trivia night, or enjoy more than one happy hour with her per week. As tempting as it all sounds, he doesn't let himself think that way. His time with his mom is precious, and it's dwindling quickly.

He wrestles with laying it all out on the table versus letting her sulk. While neither is ideal, the unsureness of where to even begin leaves him quiet and still tapping his pen.

Looking at the clock, he realizes it is time to gather his belongings and head for the airport. Other Brew lovers watch him like a hawk as he organizes his work paraphernalia and tidies up his space, waiting for the opportunity to pounce on the prime location table.

Turning to a solemn Margaret, he says, "I hate to do this, but I gotta run. I'll text you later?" he asks tentatively but optimistic.

"Yeah, for sure. I'm going to head out too. I'm sure Penelope Grace is ready to escape." A half smile peeks through at the end, easing his nerves and anxiety.

"Do you mind if we snag this from you?" a young, blond girl asks on behalf of her little posse.

"Go right ahead," Hayes says, thankful to escape the Thursday afternoon crowd.

"OMG! Thanks so much!" says one of blondie's friends.

OMG? People actually say that?

* * *

Lengthy security lines and a crowded gate result in a less-than-ideal mood for Hayes. Fond of a plan and maximum efficiencies, waiting has never been one of his strengths.

In desperate need of a pick-me-up to diffuse his short temper and kill time before his delayed flight, Hayes settles down at the airport bar. He locks eyes with one of the three bartenders bustling around, and she asks, "What can I get you, sir?"

"Coors Light. Draft," Hayes says dryly, hoping the ice-cold therapy will do the trick.

He sits slumped over with his head hanging limply and listens to the stories of nearby strangers. Some discuss their upcoming trips, while others reflect on where they have just been. Groups of friends, coworkers, and lovers. *Everyone* seems to have *someone*.

Triggered, he retrieves his phone to reach out to *his* someone. Though they haven't yet made it official, their mutual feelings are evident.

> HAYES
> *Glad we got to grab some coffee this afternoon. And would rather be spending the evening with you at Fred's :(*

> MARGARET
> *Same. What are you up to now? You left in a hurry!*

The temptation to come clean hits him hard for the second time today. But again, the uncertainty of where to begin gives him pause.

> HAYES
> *Sorry about that. Supposed to be spending the weekend with my parents, so I had to hit the road.*

Not a lie.

Taking the last swig of his first refresher, he's interrupted. "Care for another one?"

Hayes nods, dismissing the notification of yet another thirty-minute departure delay.

> MARGARET
> *Nice!*

> MARGARET
> *Wait... Does that mean you're going to Chicago? Again?*

Ugh.

The beginnings of a buzz come over him and begin to knock down his walls.

> HAYES
> *Lol, yes. I'm at the airport now. But I would give anything to be drunk at Fred's with you write now*

He presses *send* without even rereading to A) catch his typo and B) rephrase the entire message to not sound like a crazy person.

Within seconds, three little dots appear on the screen.

> MARGARET
> *Same. If only you could meet me there in fifteen;)*

> HAYES
> *If only...*

His message is already out in the universe and reading *delivered* when the automated airport intercom voice interrupts his thoughts.

"Attention passengers of United Airlines Flight 2331 to Chicago. This flight has been canceled. Please visit a gate attendant or log into the United app to reschedule."

Looking around, he mumbles, "Seriously?"

Then, motioning for the bartender, he closes out his tab with a hefty tip and an illegible signature.

Grabbing his bag, he beelines for Gate A14, even more agitated than *before* the beers. Given the flight's full capacity, the line to speak with the airline representative runs the length of the gate area.

Great.

Various combinations of friends, coworkers, and lovers from the bar stand before him in line, attempting to resolve their own issues. But one by one, they peel off with expressions of anger, frustration, and exhaustion.

Accepting he isn't making it to Chicago tonight, Hayes heads back to the parking lot he circled for a spot just a few hours before, multi-tasking along the way.

> HAYES
> *It will probably take me closer to thirty*
>
> MARGARET
> *Wait, really?*
>
> HAYES
> *Some things are just meant to be*
>
> MARGARET
> *See you soon!*

Hayes emphasizes her message before firing off another to his family group message consisting of his parents and brothers.

> HAYES
> *My flight was canceled due to the weather. Rescheduling for one in the a.m. Will be there as early as I can tomorrow... hoping 8 a.m. Keep you posted.*

Hayes contemplates driving over to Fred's, but some quick math reveals he might as well Uber since he will end up paying for the airport parking anyway. Throughout his ride, he reconfigures his weekend plans with his family via text. While part of him did want to get home and spend time with *them* tonight, another side of him was grateful to be spending it with *her*.

Spotting her Jeep from a distance, Hayes makes his way to her. The November air is crisp on his exposed skin, and the leaves crunch beneath his feet. The lights were flickering above him, and a truck honking nearby sent him back to the time they made out in the parking lot like kids, wondering if that might happen again tonight.

"You look great!" Hayes says, noticing she has changed clothes since they parted ways earlier.

"So do you. Long time no see," Margaret teases, tugging on his collared shirt playfully.

Pivoting directions to head toward the live music, Hayes casually grabs her hand like he's done it a million times before.

Where is all this impulsivity coming from?

Toasting to the end of the week and their time together, they sit under the twinkle lights, absorbing the other's company. After a couple of refills, their conversation is interrupted by a petite blond exclaiming, "Margaret! OMG!"

I guess people really do say that.

Margaret turns around and, with equal gusto, greets the bubbly blond. "Britt! I was literally just thinking on my way over how crazy it would be if we bumped into you!"

Not yet part of the conversation, Hayes glances between the women, gesturing excitedly and making googly eyes in his direction. *Oh, great.*

"Hayes, meet Britt." Shifting her gaze, Margaret reverses the introduction. "Britt, this is Hayes."

Britt continues to introduce other friends of hers to the couple. Small talk ensues, and for the first time, Hayes observes Margaret interacting with other people, her smile electric and warmth contagious. As the night draws on, the attraction builds, and Hayes finds himself pulled to her like a magnet.

Hours pass and one by one, the group starts to dwindle, leaving them how they started—alone, under the twinkle lights. Their wandering eyes and exploratory hands are telling a compelling story, but he isn't sure how it will end.

What happens now?

As they approach Margaret's car, where they first met up, Hayes shoves his hands deep in his pockets and keeps his eyes on the ground. Antsy, he fidgets and sneaks a peak at his watch.

11:24 p.m.

A solid six hours until he needs to be back at the airport.

"I—I wish the night," he says, diverting his gaze away, "didn't have to end..." As he trails off, he looks up at Margaret honestly.

Hopefully.

Pleadingly.

"Would you, uh," she hesitates and pulls at a loose string on her sweater, "want to come over?"

Her volume is low, weak, and hesitant, but it's enough. It's exactly what he wanted to hear.

Gently placing one hand on her lower back and the other at the base of her neck, Hayes pulls her in and closes the gap between them, savoring the moment.

"Yes."

CHAPTER 11

Buzzing around her bedroom like a bee at a lemonade stand, Margaret gestures to the bathroom and nightstand and instructs Hayes to make himself comfortable. He obeys as if he is the student and she is the teacher.

With Hayes out of the room, Margaret pilfers through all the drawers and baskets, racking her brain for what to wear. Weighing the pros and cons of each option, *too revealing and giving the wrong idea* or *too old-timey and also giving the wrong idea*, Margaret settles for a black silk set. While modest, at least it still leaves *something* to the imagination.

I am so out of practice.

Margaret completes her nightly routine in record time despite adding a few extra steps. Though she removes her makeup, she replaces it with an extra glow serum and under-eye cream to brighten her face and avoid looking like a zombie. She brushes the curls out of her hair but decides to add a little dry shampoo so it doesn't look oily and flat. Coating her lips in Chapstick and pinching her cheeks for added color, Margaret inhales deeply, summoning courage and calmness before opening the door.

When she reemerges, Hayes is lying down, his broad shoulders and toned stomach on full display. Because Margaret has only seen him clothed up until this point, the breath is knocked out of her. Like a sucker punch to the gut.

"H-h-hi," she stutters, rocking back on her heels, unsteady despite her hand resting on the door frame specifically for stability. Uncomfortable and exposed, Margaret slides into the bed and attempts to cover herself up.

More and more nervous with every passing second, she wished she had gone for one of the more modest pajama sets in her wardrobe, like the old college T-shirt and raggedy pair of shorts she'd contemplated before shoving them into the back of her dresser.

How close should I get to him? Are we supposed to touch? How did we end up here? When do I turn off the light? Shit, I should've turned on his lamp instead.

She flashes back to their first picnic at The Pearl, her pounding heart and racing mind panicked about where to sit on the silly blanket. It seems so trivial now.

She stares at the ceiling, wondering what she should say or do next. Margaret flicks off the lamp and pulls the covers up to her neck with a subtle huff, willing the darkness to calm her nerves.

Though she returns to her former position, something about the lack of light makes him appear closer. Much closer.

Rolling onto his side, Hayes props his head up and whispers in a raspy voice, "I had fun with you tonight."

"Me too," Margaret says softly, wiggling around, trying to find comfort.

"And your friend seemed nice. How do you know her again?"

"She actually lives in the building next door. We met in the parking lot one day and hit it off."

Margaret senses him nodding, so she continues. "Britt works crazy hours at the hospital, so we haven't gotten to hang out much. But yeah, she's nice."

Turning her head to face him, Margaret catches a whiff of his masculine scent. A good balance between earthy and sweet. She attempts to memorize how he smells. *Intoxicating.*

"Thanks for letting me come over," he says, brushing a strand of hair out of her face and gently tracing her jawline. Though it takes every ounce of her willpower, Margaret pulls her eyes from his lips and locks them with his.

With a lump in her throat, Margaret remains quiet, managing only an affirmative murmur.

Her neck aches from the awkward angle, and Margaret rolls onto her side to face him straight on. Her hands are folded underneath her chin, and they admire each other in silence. The whir of the fan and their breath are the only sounds in the room.

Shifting her gaze downward and tracing the pattern of her cheetah print sheets, Margaret feels him drawing in.

Moving closer.

And closer.

Until there is no space between them.

They collide with passion. A tangled mess of limbs and heavy breathing. Desire permeates the air and dictates their every move.

For the first time, Margaret messes with his already tousled hair and runs her hands along his muscular back. Meanwhile, his fingers dance along her skin, leaving a tingling sensation everywhere they touch.

She savors the feeling of him exploring her body with both his hands and lips, each new discovery gentler than before.

The rest is a blur. An indescribable, unimaginable blur.

Margaret falls asleep in his arms, comforted by his presence and sincerity. She dreams about *Hayes* and their deep emotional connection instead of *fake Marshall,* thankful to finally be experiencing something *real.*

When her alarm goes off, Hayes's side of the bed is empty. A stitch of sadness hits her, but she doesn't let it fester, knowing he has to get to the airport early. Instead, she replays the previous night in her mind, the corners of her lips twitching upward and her heart beating faster in response.

On her way to let Penelope out, Margaret discovers a sticky note featuring familiar typewriter-like penmanship taped to the inside of her door.

> *Sorry, I had to run... wish I could've stayed!*
> *Thank you for last night.*
> *You have no idea how much I needed it.*
> *You are something special.*
> *Let's do it again. Soon.*
> *—H*

Spinning around and pressing her back to the wall as the girls do in all the movies, Margaret clutches the note to her chest with glee. She rereads it repeatedly, in denial that *he* could think these things about *her.*

Despite attempting to go about her business and tackle her responsibilities for the day as if all is normal, Margaret can't shake the thought of Hayes. Him sleeping next to her, gently kissing her cheek, and leaving behind love notes… There's too much to ignore. He seems to penetrate her every thought.

Fortunately, though, Lacey approved a work-from-home day for everyone, giving Margaret ample time and freedom to prepare for the wedding weekend festivities. Before the out-of-towners arrive, she manages to knock out her spray tan, nail appointment, and Penelope's accommodations.

For once, being a local is paying off!

Referencing yet another detailed itinerary, this one courtesy of Caroline's wedding planner, Margaret ensures she has everything on the packing list, including a handwritten note for the bride and a bottle of booze to exchange with the groomsman she is partnered with.

Eager to see her friends and get the party going, Margaret makes her way across town to The Bella Hotel. She parks in a spot half a mile away to avoid the hefty valet fees. Lugging her belongings to the hotel lobby, Margaret checks into one of the many rooms reserved for the bridal party.

In between answering the front desk attendant's questions, Margaret observes her surroundings, like a tourist taking in Times Square for the first time. The exposed brick, genuine leather chairs, original tile flooring, and visitor-only library draw her in. The aroma from the on-site coffee shop wafts through the air as laughter erupts from the cocktail bar around the corner. Both pique her interest.

With the room keys in hand, she follows the scent of coffee beans for an afternoon treat. Instead of her usual iced americano, Margaret indulges in an oat milk latte. She sits in one of the many extravagant common areas to await the arrival of the others.

Playing out the rest of the weekend in her mind, she longs for Hayes and his company. She contemplated asking him to join her but ultimately decided against it. Between her bridesmaid duties, knowing everyone in attendance, and her assumption he already had plans, she didn't really see any other option than to fly solo.

Fortunately, or unfortunately, rather, Margaret has become accustomed to being the third, fifth, and seventh wheel over the years. It doesn't bother her near as much as it used to, but that doesn't mean she wouldn't love for Hayes to be her date.

Oh, what it would be like to prance around arm in arm, pose for photo after photo, and dance to song after song... just under different circumstances, perhaps.

> MARGARET
> *Remind me. Have you ever been to The Bella Hotel? We should totally come here for a drink sometime!*

> MR. AMERICANO/HAYES
> *I have, but only briefly. Add it to the list!*

> MARGARET
> *This is my first time here, and it is incredible! I love the modern and historic vibes!*

Struggling to capture her awe for the century-old establishment, Margaret looks around for inspiration and the appropriate words to capture its beauty. While elevated and luxurious, the hotel is still cozy and intimate, thanks to its interior design and furnishings. The perfect balance.

> MR. AMERICANO/HAYES
> *Is that where all the wedding festivities are taking place?*
>
> MARGARET
> *Yes, for the most part! I think the rehearsal dinner is technically somewhere else tonight, but still close by.*
>
> MR. AMERICANO/HAYES
> *Wish I was there with you. I'm sure you look beautiful as always.*

Though he has said similar things before, his compliments still set off fireworks inside her. To disguise her blushing smile, Margaret takes a sip of her fancy coffee, swirling the contents of the cup around for dramatic effect.

Surrounded by other individuals, couples, and groups, Margaret tries to imagine their stories and what brings them in today. Personal or professional, locals or visitors, lovers, or singles.

She pictures herself here with Hayes, treating themselves to a luxurious staycation complete with fancy meals and indulgent espresso martinis.

> MARGARET
> *I wish you were too <3*

Curled up on the worn leather couch and surrounded by plush pillows, Margaret stares at her phone. Flipping between various apps, she anxiously awaits his response, hoping for another flirty string of words that send shivers down her spine.

Despite her optimism, it doesn't come.

By the time her cup is empty, the group chat has come to life, and messages are flooding in faster than she can keep up with. Knowing her friends are set to arrive in less than ten, Margaret gathers her belongings and relocates to her room, wishing she was sharing it with someone else.

CHAPTER 12

―――

One day, that will be me.

The thought runs through Margaret's head a million times on Caroline's wedding day.

Initially, it popped into her mind mid-first look with the bridesmaids. As the photographer counted down, "Three… two… one…," Margaret and the others spun around, their jaws dropping in awe of their friend in white.

Then, as she stood next to the massive flower arch and large cross with tears in her eyes, the bride walked down the aisle toward her groom to the tune of a string quartet.

And afterward, as the newlyweds, just pronounced husband and wife, exited the ceremony space to the cheers and applause of their loved ones.

Then once more, as they entered the grandiose reception hall on the DJ's cue, the happy couple waved their hands in the air and smiled from ear to ear.

One day, that will be me.

Despite Margaret's thoughts teetering on the line of jealousy, she truly is thrilled for the new Mr. and Mrs. John Roberts. They are a perfect fit and will live a long and happy life together. Nonetheless, celebrating without spite is hard. It's like rubbing salt on an open wound.

Following an elaborate four-course meal, the happy couple engages in the traditional wedding dances with each other and their parents before ceremoniously opening the dance floor to the rest of the attendees.

The DJ reads the crowd, playing a mix of choreographed group dances, classic pump-up songs, and heartfelt slow tunes. Disco lights bounce off the walls transforming the sophisticated ballroom into a nightclub as guests flock to the center of the room, covering up the custom, monogrammed dance floor in the process.

While all her friends are waltzing with their husbands, Margaret lingers along the perimeter. She tries to play it cool as if she is *choosing* to people-watch and *really* enjoying her chardonnay, but the truth is, she feels left out.

Behind.

Alone.

Like she has no choice.

The sight of others pressed against their person makes her think of Hayes and what it would be like if he were here. Though they have never danced together, she suspects he is smooth and has a great rhythm. She imagines he would take great care of her, bringing her drink refills, keeping her laughing, and reminding her she is beautiful. She attempts to drown out the feelings of sadness and regret with another swig of wine.

One slow song gives way to another as Margaret searches for a chair to give her feet a break. On her way, she is intercepted by one of John's groomsmen.

"Would ya like to, uh, dance?" he asks with a slight hesitation in his voice and failing to make eye contact. Since the ceremony, he's lost his jacket, and his tie is cattywampus, but what the hell.

With a shrug, Margaret says, "Sure." Anything to *not* be the only person sitting on the sidelines.

It only takes one spin for her to realize the gentlemanly groomsman has already consumed one too many Jack and Cokes this evening. He's unsteady and leaning on her to stay upright. His words are slurred, and his scent is resonant of a whiskey bottle.

Margaret rolls her eyes, peering over his shoulder and attempting to minimize contact with his sweaty back. She scans the room for her friends, eager to escape this trap she walked right into. Fumbling his words and speaking incoherently, he tries to compliment Margaret's looks and ask if she has a boyfriend.

With a sassy tone, Margaret says, "Actually, I do. He just couldn't make it."

Though it might be slightly stretching the truth, the fact that his eyes are more focused on her chest than anything else gives her a hall pass.

Fortunately for Margaret, the song fizzles out a few seconds later. She breaks away, heading directly for her friends clear across the room as her former dance partner stumbles forward, tripping over his own feet.

Tess, Caroline, and Susannah appear to be huddled up and engaged in deep conversation. Given the extreme background noise, Margaret can't tell what the topic of discussion is, but based on their wild gestures, it looks juicy.

Her excitement builds, wanting the scoop and in on the drama, but as the DJ transitions from one beat to another, things change. The volume lowers, and their boisterous actions and loud voices cannot be mistaken. Her insides churn as it becomes crystal clear that they are talking about *her*.

She sees them, but they haven't yet spotted her. With crossed arms and stinging eyes, Margaret listens as each and every word cuts her like a dagger.

"I just don't understand how she can think this is a good idea. She literally knows nothing about him!" Tess says, shaking her head. "It seems like a disaster waiting to happen."

The others nod and Susannah adds, "I think she's just desperate. I think she is lonely and looking for companionship. I can't blame her, but it doesn't seem like this is the best solution..." She trails off, metaphorically passing the mic to Caroline.

"I'm surprised she doesn't see these red flags and have problems with them too... like he is gone all the time. She hasn't met any of his friends or family or anything!" Caroline's hands fall to her sides in exasperation, and she turns enough to catch a glimpse of Margaret retreating.

She hears them calling out for her, but it's too late.

A mix of heartbreak and fury stirs within her as tears trickle down her face and beads of sweat build on her palms.

How could they talk about me like that?

My best friends.

Their words echo in her mind. *Disaster. Desperate. Lonely. Red flags.*

Locked in a bathroom stall, Margaret blots her cheeks with a fancy bathroom hand towel and touches up her makeup.

She studies her reflection in the mirror and gives herself an internal pep-talk.

They don't even know him. You aren't desperate. Follow your heart and stay true to yourself.

Taking one final deep breath, Margaret prepares to face the music. Literally. The door opens before she even reaches for the handle, revealing none other than the culprits themselves. *Of course.*

"Margaret…" Tess begins. "Listen. It isn't what you think."

Margaret raises her eyebrows in both recognition and awe, shrugs, and shakes her head.

Really? That's all?

While a million thoughts rush through her head, Margaret remains quiet, allowing her silence to speak for her. Staring them down and transferring her weight, she ponders the pros and cons of hashing it all out right here and now.

Looking at her best friends, all she sees are deer in headlights. She can sense the shock and pain, but is there remorse? For what they said or just that they were caught? Betrayal washes over her and triggers her desire to escape as she concludes now isn't the time.

Margaret shimmies past her friends without uttering a word. Though she hears Susannah quietly call out her name with more sadness than anything in her voice, Margaret doesn't stop. Instead, she keeps walking, refusing to provide them with the satisfaction of a response or acknowledgment.

Margaret attempts to make the most of the rest of the evening, conversing with other guests she likely wouldn't have otherwise spoken to. While she doesn't outright talk to Tess, Susannah, or Caroline, she doesn't overtly ignore them either. Their tone and posture tell her enough—this will be revisited later.

Following the bride and groom's departure, Margaret slips out a side exit and scurries home, not in the mood for any more drama tonight. She ditches her bridesmaid dress in the corner and scrubs off her overpriced makeup with fury before slipping into bed.

Despite all the lights being off, the ceiling is still illuminated by the glow of her phone. She continues to hear *Bzz. Bzz. Bzz.* Over and over and over.

Rolling onto her side, she covers her head with the pillow to escape the sound, but when that doesn't work, she snatches the phone instead with the intent to activate the Do Not Disturb feature.

In the process, she discovers a message from Mr. Americano and lacks the self-control to ignore it.

> MR. AMERICANO/HAYES
> *I hope you had a great night! Can't wait to hear all about it*

And, for the first time ever, he includes a kiss emoji. Not that she needs anything else to further complicate the relationship—or lack thereof.

Oh, Hayes. If only you knew.

Bzz. Bzz. Bzz.

Notifications continue to come through. While it's only Tess and Susannah in the group chat, they speak on behalf of Caroline too. Apologies, reasons, and excuses for their collective behavior. Pleas for forgiveness and the chance to make it up to her.

Margaret leaves them on read and falls asleep with her phone in her hand. The following morning, she is awoken by their calls.

Decline.

The *Bzz. Bzz. Bzz.* continues and, finally, Margaret relents.

After exchanging a few texts, they agree to meet at a bakery nearby before they all go their separate directions. While Tess and Susannah are just going home, Caroline will be embarking on a three-week European escapade with her new husband later this evening, and she is begging to resolve their differences beforehand.

Margaret's perfectly timed arrival allows her to catch them pouring out of Susannah's new "mom car," with no significant others in tow. Margaret swallows deeply, knowing "no-boys-allowed" means things are about to get serious.

"Hey, pretty lady!" Tess exclaims with arms outstretched, expecting a hug.

"Good morning," Margaret says with less inflection. "Did you guys let Sus practice buckling you in the backseat?" Despite her flat and sarcastic tone, the dry humor is well received.

"Ha! Ha! I asked her to, but she refused… I thought about throwing a fit!" Caroline jokes, always one to play along with the silly games and antics.

"This place is adorable!" Susannah says. "So glad we're giving it a try. The boys decided to squeeze in a round of golf before we leave, so we're not in a rush."

Oh, great.

The bakery's interior has classic café vibes, featuring pastel and neutral decor on the walls. Original square tiles cover the floor, and well-trained pastry chefs shuffle back and forth in the distance. A light dusting of flour coats the entire kitchen, making it feel both authentic and well-loved. The café attracts patrons of all ages and backgrounds, all two dozen or so seats currently occupied.

"I wish my kitchen smelled like this!" Susannah says, wafting the fresh baked goods scent around and savoring the sweetness.

Once at the counter, their order spills out like a shopping list. While the others order frilly drinks, Margaret opts for her staple iced americano, thinking of Hayes as the words escape her mouth. Her hands are clammy as a result of her anxiety about what the next few minutes will entail.

A table becomes available just as the barista puts the finishing touches on their lavish lattes. At the back of the pack, Margaret is left with the seat facing the window... and her three friends. They've strategically positioned themselves to look toward her—like an interview. Or an intervention. Or an interrogation.

Are they really doing this right now?

Her eyes dart to the door, and her heart rate increases. Margaret shifts in her seat uncomfortably, already contemplating her escape route. She waits for someone else to talk first, unwilling to open up this can of worms or intentionally put herself in the hot seat. Though it seems she might already be there.

"Margaret..." Tess begins, poised and professional, as if this *is* an interview. "We are so sorry for what happened last night. No excuses."

Caroline picks up the imaginary talking stick and continues. "We don't want to see you get hurt or heartbroken. Ever. We want to protect you. Based on what you have told us about Hayes, we just have some concerns. We should have talked to you first... not each other."

"Please forgive us. We want the best for you... for you to be happy and loved and cared for. You are a rockstar!" Susannah says with jazz hands. "And you deserve someone who treats you as such. No games. No lies." She finishes the relay for them.

So they coordinated this. Probably practiced in the mom car. Cute.

A few awkward beats pass, with the clanging of baking sheets and small talk from surrounding tables filling the silence.

Margaret looks up but doesn't speak.

"Look, I think we have questions and concerns that make us worry you might get hurt. Does that make sense?" Tess asks.

Margaret nods.

"We haven't met him. And let's be honest, you haven't shared *too* much about him either. Do you know where he lives? Has he told you *anything* specific about his life?"

Margaret shrugs and lets out an exasperated sigh.

"What does that even mean?" Tess bursts out with confusion and frustration, her hands flying up in the air.

Margaret freezes, trying to grasp the fact that her best friend just raised her voice and triggered the rise of an imaginary wall around her.

"I'm sorry. That was uncalled for," Tess apologizes, scooting her chair back for a little more distance.

"I think what Tess was trying to say is there are just some red flags we think you should be aware of…" Caroline pauses, gauging Margaret's reaction to see if this approach is gaining traction. "You don't have to stop seeing him. We think there are some things you should think about. It might be hard to grasp the big picture when you're so close to it, ya know?"

Margaret nods again. Caroline's buzz words trigger the pain of last night, leaving her to believe silence is still her only friend in this situation.

Caroline continues, "For example, have you ever hung out with him on the weekend? He seems to travel a lot. Do you think that's weird?"

Defensively, Margaret says, "It's for work."

"He travels for his job on the weekends only? That doesn't sound right. I thought you said you guys had worked together at that coffee shop a few times?" she challenges.

"Yeah, we have." Seeing her point, Margaret shifts her position, crossing her arms and legs as yet another defense mechanism.

"So, does that not make you wonder what he's doing on the weekends? Where he's going? Who he's with?" Caroline continues while the others sit quietly and patiently.

"I guess. But I'm sure there is an explanation," Margaret justifies with little conviction.

Sighing, Caroline presses harder. "Margaret, listen to yourself. You basically only know what he has told you with no evidence, proof, or substantiation. If it were one of us in this position, you would be freaking out and quoting a true crime podcast episode or something about how dangerous it is to date strangers that you don't have any mutual connections with…" She trails off as Margaret visibly collapses in her chair, her head down and back arched, accepting defeat.

She isn't wrong. What am I doing? What the hell *am I doing?*

"Does he have social media? Can you corroborate anything he's told you?" Caroline asks again.

She did do some research when they first met but couldn't find anything more than an outdated Facebook profile with a profile picture from 2016. This realization is enough to break her silence. "You're right. I don't know what I'm doing." It's like the walls cave in around her, revealing her fairytale is a farce.

"We aren't trying to hurt you. And I'm sorry if we have. I want to protect you—just like you would do for me or any one of us," Tess says, much cooler than before.

Still refusing to make eye contact, Margaret nods in acknowledgment and wipes her cheek with a crumb-covered pastry napkin, reminding her of that fateful day and his damn typewriter penmanship.

CHAPTER 13

———

"Ladies and gentlemen," the flight attendant says with her head up and shoulders back, "The pilot anticipates some turbulence ahead. Please remain in your seat with your seatbelt fastened. We will provide another update as soon as possible. Thank you for your understanding and patience."

The microphone clicks at the end, sending a ripple of grumbles through the plane.

Given his flight fiasco a few days ago, Hayes opted for the later flight today to make up for it. However, his late departure has him cutting it closer than he'd like for his typical Sunday evening hangout at The Pearl with Margaret.

After a few minutes, another announcement comes through. "Ladies and gentlemen, this is your captain speaking. We've adjusted our route to avoid the weather. It shouldn't be too bumpy for you, but it will take a little longer to reach our destination. Sit back, relax, and enjoy the flight. We'll get you to San Antonio International Airport as soon as possible!"

Fellow passengers sigh with understanding frustration before returning to their books, podcasts, and predownloaded

TV shows. Glancing at his watch, Hayes is antsy, his knee bouncing up and down nervously.

Unfortunately, this airplane is not equipped with the latest and greatest Wi-Fi technology, so he can't shoot Margaret a text. Though he is confident she will understand, he still feels like an ass.

Accepting the circumstances are out of his control, he resolves to apologize profusely later. Having hardly slept in the last forty-eight hours, Hayes attempts to rest and relax.

When his brain refuses to shut off, he stares out the window instead. The skyline, with characteristics of a professional watercolor painting courtesy of the setting sun and thunderstorms in the distance, brings him peace. He admires the tumultuous clouds responsible for the bumpiness and delay. He draws an ironic parallel to all the other clouds in his life—uncontrollable events and situations that continue to cause chaos and setbacks.

His time in reflection leaves him with four key points at the top of his mind.

- *Time is precious and fleeting.*
- *I need to make the most of my time with those I care about—Mom, Dad, my brothers, Margaret, etc.*
- *I need to tell Margaret what's going on. It isn't fair for her not to get to know the whole me. I hope she's understanding.*
- *Promotion or not, I need to work on my work-life balance.*

As the plane makes contact with the runway, he reconnects his cell, and it immediately begins to buzz.

> MARGARET, 5:48 p.m.
> *Hey! We're still on for tonight, right?*

MARGARET, 5:59 p.m.
See you in fifteen? Same place as usual?

MARGARET, 6:24 p.m.
I've been out and about all day, so I think I'm gonna head home. Hope everything's okay.

His alarm bells go off, and panic sets in.

HAYES, 7:02 p.m.
I'm so sorry. My flight was rerouted midway. Just landed and waiting to deplane. Can I still see you? I promise I'll be there as soon as possible.

He sees her typing, but nothing comes through.

When the "seatbelt" light is no longer illuminated, Hayes becomes the person he hates, springing up in a rush to be the first one off the plane. Given his window seat status, he's held back by the other, more patient passengers in his row. When the opportunity finally presents itself to slide by, grab his bag from the overhead bin and run, he does.

He doesn't slow down once through the gates, around the food court, or down the stairs past baggage claim.

With a precise ETA and extreme guilt, Hayes opts to call Margaret. The phone rings and rings, and he longs to hear her voice. When it never connects, he's left listening to an automated voice with no choice but to record a message or hang up.

"Hey," Hayes says, winded from his dead sprint. "I'm really sorry about tonight. We ran into bad weather and had to reroute. Anyway, I feel horrible about it, and I'd still like to see you. Can I maybe bring dinner or ice cream or something? Let me know, and I'll do it. Bye."

Hanging up, he is hit with the feeling that something is different.

Off. Not quite right.

Behind the wheel and in motion, he heads in Margaret's direction on the off-chance he hears from her. As Hayes weaves his way out of the airport, dodging shuttles and merging lanes, she responds.

At first, he is relieved, but it doesn't last long...

> MARGARET
> *No worries. I'm already at home in my pajamas, lol*

His relief is replaced quickly with concern and confusion.

What does that mean? Yes? No? Maybe?

Frustrated by the crypticness, Hayes turns up the volume and rolls down the window as a distraction.

> MARGARET
> *but you know I don't say no to ice cream;)*

Oh, thank goodness.

> HAYES
> *Be there in ten*

Having discussed their ice cream preferences at length during their first date, Hayes knows what he needs to make up for his poor planning skills. Whipping into the nearby grocery store, he throws the truck in park and resumes his jog from earlier, this time in the direction of the frozen department.

Scanning the ice cream aisle like a crossword puzzle, he narrows in on a pint of Candy Bar. Though he's never had it, the contents of the cardboard carton could not be better, according to the ice cream extraordinaire herself.

Retracing his steps to the front of the store, Hayes does a quick pivot, opting to upgrade to a half-gallon. And, with an uneasy feeling still churning in his gut, he also makes the split decision to grab an apology card to complement the sweet treat.

"I've seen this combination before…" the checker comments, eyeing the ice cream and card combo. "Rough day?"

Nodding and running a hand through his hair, Hayes says, "Yeah, you could say that."

Minutes later, he's standing outside Margaret's door. In the seconds between his knuckles making rapid contact with the frame and Margaret turning the knob, he wishes he'd thought more critically about what he was going to say and how he would handle this situation.

Shit.

Hayes embraces her, hoping that the gentle squeeze of his arms and beating heart against her chest will mean something. "Hi," he whispers into her neck. "I'm so sorry about tonight…"

"It's okay. I understand. It's not like you can control the weather though that would be cool…"

Despite her attempt at humor and dismissive language, her tone isn't persuasive. It's flat and skeptical, as if she doesn't quite buy it.

"Thank you for understanding. And for letting me come over…" He moves through the apartment as if he's walking on eggshells. Reaching the kitchen island, Hayes pulls the carton out of the red and white grocery bag, the crinkling of plastic dramatized by the dense silence.

"You remembered!" Margaret says with both excitement and shock in her voice. Seeing her light up finally puts the doubts lingering in Hayes's mind at ease. Her bright smile and genuine joy set off fireworks inside him.

This is the Margaret I missed.

"I mean, not that I didn't think you would or anything…" she says with a hint of sarcasm. Busying herself with bowls and spoons, she inquires more about his travels, clearly fishing for information.

Hayes gives her the lowdown on all that's happened since he snuck out without disturbing her or Penelope Grace Friday morning. He shares the high points—spending time with his mom and dad, helping out around the house, and preparing their meals. All of which was true and did happen—just not for the reasons she might expect.

Truthfully, he'd hardly slept and spent most of his time at the hospital in a corner room, courtesy of his doctor brother. Test after test, consult after consult, continuously seeking answers and hope.

During nonvisitor hours, he *was* at home completing chores—cleaning out the gutters, running the laundry, and meal prepping. He and his brothers had a few conference calls to proactively discuss the logistics of their mother's care, recognizing that the improvement they had long hoped for may never come.

Viewing their time together as an escape from reality, he leaves out the emotional details, refusing to focus on himself or his vulnerabilities.

She smiles as he speaks about his family. "Aw, are you going to be the winner of the best son award this year?" she asks.

"I didn't realize such an award existed. But if it did, I doubt I'd be the recipient," he says, playing along.

Scooping each of them a heaping bowl full of ice cream, Margaret remains silent. Her furrowed brow stirs up more anxiety, leading him to believe there is something she isn't saying.

They relocate to the couch, and Penelope Grace joins them, hoping to get lucky and earn a sweet treat of her own. They eat in silence, other than the occasional rustle of pillows and the sound of metal spoons clinking the sides of their bowls.

While he can't quite put his finger on it, something is not right. Determined to get to the bottom of it, he starts with an easy question. "So, how was the wedding? I want to hear all about it!"

Hugging her knees, Margaret seems to tense up even more.

Not part of the plan.

"It was beautiful! Pretty fun, too," she says.

That's it?

"The Bella Hotel is so awesome. How was it being back together with everyone?"

Slipping stray strands of hair behind her ear and sighing, Margaret says, "Pretty good. A little weird though, honestly."

Rotating to face her more straight on, Hayes probes again. "Weird? How so? I thought y'all were besties?"

She bites her lip and nods. When she finally says, "Me too," her voice cracks and a single tear trickles down her face. She tries to cover it up by tending to their empty bowls, but there's no point.

Hayes, sensing much on her mind and at the tip of her tongue, decides to bite the bullet. Unsure of what to say or ask to give her the platform she needs to open up, he simply says, "Is everything okay? Do you wanna talk about it?"

Returning to the couch, she sits farther away this time on the third cushion rather than straddling the second.

She motions to speak, but nothing comes out. Her eyes move from her knees to the throw pillows and his hands before finally making it anywhere near his face. "I just…"

Hayes remains quiet and still, nodding ever so slightly.

"I really like you. But I have some questions. Some hesitations," she finally admits.

He nods, more definitively this time, uneasy about the direction the conversation is heading.

"First of all, what are we?"

Leaning back a little farther on the couch and gently rubbing the stubble on his jaw, Hayes contemplates her question and the answer, both of which make him apprehensive.

Folding one leg under the other and propping his head up on the couch, he says, "Well, I really like you too. I've enjoyed every minute we've spent together. You're fun, ambitious, smart, creative, beautiful—everything I would be looking for." He speaks slowly and calculated.

Looking at him from the corner of her eye, Margaret asks, "*Would* be? What the hell does that mean?" Her tone is slightly more high-pitched and defensive.

"When we met at The Brew, I wouldn't say I was *looking* for someone. For a relationship. To fall in love… whatever. I'm not exactly at a point in my life where that is an option…"

Hayes trails off, telling the truth but not wanting to overemphasize the gravity of his message.

Margaret is now looking up at him with what can only be described as pleading puppy dog eyes. She waits patiently for him to continue.

Accepting his fate that he got them into this predicament and needs to get them out of it, Hayes continues. "I just can't commit to a relationship right now. I wish I could. I *do* have feelings for you and if I were to be in a relationship, I would only want it to be with *you*, Margaret," he says, squeezing both of her perfectly manicured hands.

Her facial expression has yet to change. Firm and stone-cold, the only shimmer is in her glossy eyes.

"And you're just now figuring this out?" she asks, her expression fallen and gaze downcast.

"I want this to be something, but I've got a lot going on, and I don't think I can give you what you deserve."

Knowing she is slipping through his fingers, Hayes holds her hands tighter, angry with himself for letting her go so easily.

"I still don't understand. Why can't we just try? I feel like this is coming out of nowhere," she says.

Drawing in a deep breath and shifting his hands to rest on her knees, Hayes says, "Margaret… Please don't hate me for what I am about to tell you…"

CHAPTER 14

"I haven't exactly been completely honest with you…"

Margaret's heart, beating like a drum, and her mind, racing like a horse in the Kentucky Derby, were not prepared for those words to spill out of Hayes's mouth.

A million questions swirl in her brain. Margaret can't help but think *they were right.*

She suppresses the thought of her friends, anxious to know the truth and frustrated for being lied to for months. "Just spit it out. What the hell is going on?"

"I do-don't," he stutters and fidgets before continuing, "actually live he—"

"You've got to be kidding me!" Margaret interrupts, her jaw practically on the floor.

With a head tilt, he begins again, seemingly annoyed by her lack of patience. "Well, the project I am on currently was supposed to be temporary. I was supposed to be long gone by now. But it's proven to be a lot more complicated, so I'm still here. Obviously."

She nods, struggling to understand what he is *actually* saying.

"These days, I'm spending a lot of time here, but technically Chicago is home…"

Margaret sinks into the couch, her fingers pressing into her temples, hoping the pressure will help her comprehend. After a few beats, with panic rising in her chest, she says, "Don't tell me there's someone else…"

"Of course not, Margaret. Why would you even think that?" he asks, his face contorted with emotion.

"Well," she says, casually looking around the room and letting the unusualness of the circumstances speak for themself. "I mean, I don't know what else you haven't been telling me or what other details you chose to leave out."

Shifting his position on the couch again, Hayes says, "Look." His tone is firm and intense while his hands emphasize each word. "It's only you. I promise. The truth is that I travel for work and even though I'm here a lot, Chicago is home. That's it."

"So that's why you're 'busy' all the time…" she says, using air quotes and shaking her head in disbelief.

"Yes," Hayes confirms.

The conviction in his voice makes her want to believe him, but the doubt still lingers.

Running her hands through her hair and gesturing wildly, she asks, "Why couldn't you just say so from the beginning? I don't understand!"

She watches him stare holes through the carpet and fiddle with his watch. "I don't know. I guess because I didn't know how long I would be here or how long this project would last…" The elongated pause puts a lump in her throat.

Is he referring to me as a project?

Thankfully, he continues before she can vocalize her annoyance and confusion. "But I didn't want that to keep you from giving me a shot."

Feeling like a balloon that has lost its helium, Margaret deflates. She stands and paces the length of the kitchen.

When she finally stops moving, she props herself up against the island and picks at her nails. "I can't believe this." She lets out a fake laugh, further emphasizing her disdain.

Her heart is filled with dread, but her mind longs for answers. Terrified of what she might hear, she summons the courage to ask for clarification anyway. "So, what exactly are you saying?"

"I don't know, Margaret. I like you. A lot." He walks toward her with purpose. "And I like where this is going," he adds, only standing a few feet away. "But…"

"But what?" she pushes, her head falling backward and arms swinging against her sides in exasperation. "What?" she asks with more emphasis. "I *really* hope you have a good excuse."

He shakes his head and looks out the window, avoiding eye contact. "I can't make any promises."

Her stomach plummets, and she suddenly regrets the extra scoop of ice cream she ingested only minutes ago. "Again, what does that even *mean*?"

Frustration is woven into her every word.

His palms open and facing upward, he shrugs, looking totally defeated.

The lack of explanation causes her irritation to multiply. Margaret walks around to the other side of the kitchen and proceeds to tidy up, ruminating on her next move. Meanwhile, Hayes retreats to the couch, his brow furrowed and posture much less confident than normal.

Perched nervously on the edge of his seat, Hayes continues. "Sometimes the travel is predictable and planned. Sometimes it is totally random. I've tried to get into a routine because the more time I spend here, the more I get to see you."

He looks up at her across the room, hope and desperation seeping through his words. "But the truth is, they could pull me off this project tomorrow. I could be moved literally anywhere!"

She nods her head slowly but dismisses the details he just shared. "Would you like some water or something?"

"Sure, thank you."

She weighs her options for follow-up questions, focusing on the whole truth and nothing but the truth as if he is a witness in a high-profile trial. Despite her curiosity being at an all-time high, she is still hesitant to know what else he's been withholding.

With her head down and all her weight on the countertop, Margaret finally asks, "Is there anything else I should know?" She looks up, expecting him to nod and pile on even more secrets.

"Everything else I've told you is true," he says as she plops down on the couch, handing him one of the waters. "I have two older brothers. I am an uncle to three little girls, a fourth on the way. My parents mean the world to me. In fact, technically, I still live with them."

Margaret clings to the one thing she can relate to. "Sometimes I wish I still lived at home with my parents." A wave of homesickness washes over her at the thought of them, eager for the holidays and quality time. "It would make things so much easier."

"Yeah, it's not that bad. I enjoy our time together, and I do what I can to help. Like I mentioned earlier, I try to cook, keep things organized, take care of home projects for them, and whatnot." Margaret notices him take a hurried sip of water and clear his throat but doesn't let herself read further into it.

Instead, she cracks a smile. "Such a handyman."

They share a half-laugh, but it quickly fizzles out. Both of them shift nervously on the couch, folding themselves in an alternative way, avoiding all contact.

"So…" Margaret says, wiping a bead of sweat from her water glass. "You didn't really answer my question." When she looks up at him, his expression is quizzical. "I get that everything you have said is true, but you didn't confirm there isn't anything *else* you've been hiding."

Hayes sighs, leaning back again, his legs outstretched in front of him. His eyes, focused straight ahead, are sharp enough to drill a hole in the wall.

"Nope," he says. "That's it." Though his tone is as firm and persuasive as before, Margaret is still suspicious.

She leaves the floor open, allowing the painful silence to linger and forcing herself to be patient. When he doesn't budge or divulge, Margaret says, "I don't understand why you're so anti…" she pauses, searching for the right word, "us…"

"I don't know." He caves, folding into himself, a sob threatening to escape. His elbows rest on his knees and his head shakes as he tries to explain his fears and hesitations. "I haven't been in a relationship in years, Margaret. *Years!*" His gestures emphasize the timeline, embarrassment laced within them. He briefly explains some of his past trauma and the lingering side effects.

Struggling to process it all, Margaret catches something about a high school girl friend in an accident and another instance possibly related to infidelity. He continues before she's able to unpack his relationship history.

"I just don't know if I can give you all that you need," he confesses, his words wreaking havoc in her heart. "You deserve the very best. Way better than someone like me who can't even manage to be honest." The crack in his voice eases Margaret's concern that she is the only one carrying this burden.

What little air was left in her balloon dissipates. Margaret strokes Penelope Grace's head, feeling the heaviness of the situation.

"Involved? That's it? That's all you think we are?"

"Margaret." He reaches over and lays a hand on her thigh. "I didn't mean it like that. Bad word choice on my part," he says apologetically.

He stares at her. While his lips are parted like he's about to speak, he remains motionless before finally clarifying. "I meant to say I don't know that I can get any deeper into this and still be able to walk away."

Her shoulders droop, and she tilts her head back to hide her glistening eyes. "I'm not following. You're not making sense…"

His posture changes again, drawing Margaret's eyes away from Penelope Grace and to him. She studies his features intently as he looks everywhere but at her. "What I'm trying to say is my feelings for you are real. And deep. And I don't think I can just let you go. But I also don't know how to do this. I don't normally *do* relationships."

"*Mhmm*," Margaret mumbles, trying to parse out the truth from the bullshit. "So, where does that leave us?"

"I don't know," Hayes says, inching his way closer. "But what I do know is that I don't want to give up before we even try."

His lips are inches from hers, and his hands are exploring her body. "How does that sound to you?" he whispers in her ear between kisses along her neck.

Margaret pulls away, unwilling to give in so easily. *It sounds great, but you have to be realistic, Margaret.*

"What?" Hayes asks with confusion on his face.

"If you don't *do relationships*, what are we even doing here?" She throws his words back at him so he understands the pain they inflicted.

"I don't know what to do, Margaret. I don't know how to handle this. It is all foreign to me, but I want to figure it out for you. For *us*."

"Really?" she asks, craving another ounce of affirmation.

"I promise."

CHAPTER 15

———

Dressed in freshly laundered business casual with his bag slung over his shoulder and a cup of coffee in hand, Hayes leaves home, unintentionally letting the door slam behind him. Departing at precisely 7:45 a.m., he manages to beat the morning rush hour traffic, weave through the office lobby, and wave at the front desk attendants without slowing down once. He doesn't linger or chat like he normally does, determined to keep his eyes solely focused on the prize.

He chooses to climb the six flights of stairs rather than risk having to engage in elevator small talk. His head bowed and headphones in, Hayes remains in the zone, refusing to let anything throw him off his game.

Today is one he has been working toward since joining the firm eight years ago. Hayes is hopeful that all the overtime hours, headaches, stress, and extra travel days will finally pay off. Though he has developed and progressed far faster than others with his qualifications, there is still no guarantee. Becoming a partner is an unheard-of feat at his age.

The benefits of life as a partner play in his mind like a movie trailer. Calling all the shots, managing his own team rather than just being part of one, and finally having a place that really feels like home. Less traveling. More stability. *Finally.*

Hayes busies himself with small, mindless tasks during the morning hours, reserving all his brain power and sharp thinking for 11:00 a.m. The clock seems to be ticking slower today, each minute feeling more like an hour. Despite brainstorming every question and scenario that could be thrown his way, he suddenly wishes he'd spent more time preparing. How? He's not sure. But there is no such thing as being over-prepared.

As a last-ditch effort, Hayes skims over the months' worth of podcast lessons he jotted down in the notes app on his phone. Refreshing himself on leadership tactics, the performance management cycle, and key feedback loops, he thinks about all the flights and car rides he's dedicated to this very moment. While they weren't all glamorous or pleasant, he hopes they will at least have been worth it.

At 10:57, he stands, straightens his tie, and buttons his special occasion blazer. Pivoting from his desk, Hayes heads for the door with his portfolio tucked under his arm. As he crosses the threshold, his phone rings.

He contemplates letting it go to voicemail, justifying that whatever *it* is can wait. But with a few minutes to spare, he reconsiders and answers without even looking at the screen.

"Hello?" he asks.

"Hayes…" the voice on the other end gasps.

Taken aback, he recognizes the voice as familiar but in distress.

"You need to get home."

Triggered by those five words, Hayes pulls the phone away from his ear to find *Wes Thompson* on the screen.

Oh, no. Mom.

"Something bad has happened, and you need to get here. As soon as possible," Wes continues, his voice off. Shaky, scared, and almost unrecognizable.

In the background, Hayes hears nothing but chaos. Multiple voices, various beeping sounds, and sirens wailing. Panic rushes through his veins as context clues validate Wes's off-kilter demeanor.

Struggling to get a grip on reality, Hayes feebly asks, "Wes? What's wrong?"

He takes a deep breath, dreading the answer he's feared receiving since his mom's diagnosis almost four years ago. Considering their most recent weekend stint together in the hospital, it's no surprise the end is near. Despite all the warning signs, that doesn't make it any easier.

Wes sighs deeply, his voice even more fragile than before. "It's Dad."

Hayes fumbles with his phone, utterly shocked and blindsided.

A concoction of questions, curses, and anxiety swirl around in his head. His legs are no longer capable of supporting both him and the weight of the world on his shoulders. Hayes collapses back into his chair and retrieves his phone from the floor with a shattered screen. Putting Wes on speakerphone and resting his head in his hands, Hayes mumbles, "This can't be happening." Rocking nervously, he attempts to ask for clarity.

"Dad? What do you mean? What happened to him? I thought you were talking about Mom?" He can hear the denial in his own voice.

It isn't supposed to be this way.

He rubs his sweaty palms along the tops of his legs, both bouncing up and down anxiously.

"We don't know. A stroke, maybe? You just—"

"A stroke?" Hayes repeats, his heart breaking. "Oh, god, Wes. No...." He trails off, the emotions and gravity of the situation finally catching up.

"You just need to get here." While Wes has always performed well under pressure, Hayes tends to crumble, relying on his big brother and mentor for emotional support and guidance.

He scrolls through his flight options, unable to even process what is on the screen before him as Wes provides what few details they know at this time. "Sam is trying to get some more tests done. He's got us the best doctor in the city, but it's not looking good."

Clicking *confirm* on the next direct flight, Hayes grabs his bag and throws it over his shoulder. "I'm on my way. I'll be there as soon as I can." A lump lodged in his throat. Hayes is barely able to add, "Love you, bro."

Numb to the world around him, Hayes navigates his way through the office. Everything is a blur, lacking definition and humanity.

His coworkers' voices sound like static TVs, incoherent and ignorable. It isn't until he rounds the corner in front of the primary conference room that things come into focus. He steals a quick glance at his watch, which reads 11:00 on the dot.

As he approaches, the smiles and laughter of his leadership team fade, quickly replaced with expressions of worry and concern.

"You all right, Hayes?" Shawn, his longtime boss and friend inquires.

"You don't look too great," Linda, their admin, adds, grabbing his arm and guiding him to the nearest chair.

Hayes continues to stare forward, light-headed. Though he can feel his coworkers buzzing around compassionately and hear their rapid-fire questions, the only words he can muster are "dad" and "home."

Rubbing his shoulder, Linda attempts to interpret his fragmented communication. "Something's happened with your dad? You need to go home? Is that right, Hayes?" Her motherly care and comforting tone provide a sense of peace that he can acknowledge with a limp nod.

Shawn says, "All right, we can make that happen. We will get you there right away." He studies Hayes before shifting his gaze to the others. "I can take him to the airport now... I don't think he ought to be driving."

"Tha-thank you all," Hayes says, making an effort to stand though his legs are still unsteady.

Shaking their heads and offering words of comfort, his team expresses a series of well wishes. Shawn leads him out of the building and chauffeurs Hayes to the airport.

Upon arrival, Hayes thanks Shawn profusely for the ride and his understanding, the words flowing though still slightly incoherent.

"Take care of yourself, man. Let us know if we can do anything."

"Will do. Thanks, Shawn," Hayes says, tapping the top of the car and turning to walk inside.

"Hey, Hayes," Shawn calls out, "I want you to focus on your family. Don't you dare worry about anything at all here... You will be a partner when you get back."

For the first time since he picked up his brother's frantic call, Hayes feels grounded and cognizant. Like himself. Though the sense of relief is fleeting, he clings to it like a life raft in the middle of the ocean.

He manages a half smile and tosses Shawn a wave, leaving the details and his excitement unspoken.

Hayes races through security, thanking his lucky stars for TSA PreCheck, and high-tails it to his gate in record time. He approaches just as the line to board has died down, allowing him to strut right on as the last passenger aboard flight 728. He rifles through his bag to locate his boarding pass and hands it to the gate attendant.

"Right on time, sir. Have a great flight," she says, closing the door behind him.

Hayes finds his seat on the third row of the plane, appreciating the ease of travel when luggage-less. Finally able to breathe, the stress of the last thirty minutes somewhat dissipating, he digs into his pocket to text Wes about his flight plans.

Except his phone isn't there. Again, he shuffles through his work bag. Also, phoneless. He double-checks both places again.

No luck.

Because the flight attendants are already giving their spiels about seatbelts, oxygen masks, and exit rows, he knows it's a lost cause. While a less-than-ideal situation, he resolves to send Wes an old-fashioned email once they reach 10,000 feet. Better than nothing.

Once given permission by the captain, Hayes retrieves his bag and pulls out his laptop.

> HAYES, 12:24 p.m.
> Hey. Lost my phone at security but on the plane and headed your way. ETA about 2:15. Meet you at the hospital?

At the sight of his company logo on the front of his laptop, Hayes plays Shawn's parting comments on repeat. *"You will be a partner when you get back."* Under any other circumstances, he would be beaming with pride and excitement, ready to pop the champagne and celebrate. A well-deserved, hard-earned achievement recognized by their entire office and department.

But instead, his mind is jumbled, full of pain, fear, and anxiety for his parents, brothers, and, selfishly, himself too. Though he has envisioned the "you need to come home" call more times than he cares to admit, it's always been in relation to his mom. Having experienced many highs and even more lows on her stage-four breast cancer journey, it never crossed his mind that something could happen to his dad, who was strong-willed, determined, and active.

How? One parent's health and well-being are enough to worry about. How am I supposed to handle two?

His eyes were stinging, and his chest was tightening. He attempts to take a nap. He didn't sleep well last night, given the stress he was under, and it's unlikely tonight will be much better.

Drifting off, his heart rate slows and panic eases. The woes of work and life no longer plague him. His conscience travels to a happy, carefree place with sandy beaches and sunny skies, a drink in his hand, and Margaret by his side.

Jolting back to consciousness, he mutters, "Oh, no. Margaret."

CHAPTER 16

Margaret has lost count of how many days it has been since she has spoken to or seen Hayes.

It feels like a lifetime.

While their "what-are-we" conversation didn't quite end with a crystal clear answer or well-defined next steps, they had at least resolved to give it a try before throwing in the towel, hadn't they? And they agreed to trust their feelings, regardless of the logistics or what-ifs, right?

Hayes slept over and wrote her another note as he slipped out before sunrise the following morning. They texted like normal, flirting, making plans, and finding excuses to see one another. The sight of his name popping up on her screen brought a smile to her face each and every time.

But then Mr. Americano up and vanished.

So much for giving it a try...

Sitting in the bathtub, her legs propped up on the ledge and a bath bomb fizzing around her, Margaret tries to pinpoint what exactly went wrong. With the cupcake fragrance swirling around her, she scrolls through her recent texts and contemplates whether she should send another.

MARGARET
Hi, there! Your big meeting was yesterday, right? How'd it go? Can't wait to hear all about it!

MARGARET
Hey! Britt invited us to go to Wurstfest this weekend! Wanted to see if you'd be interested? Thought it might be fun :)

MARGARET
Hey, stranger! I hope things are going well! Wanna grab a drink after work?

Considering every message she has mustered the courage to send so far has gone unanswered, Margaret resists the temptation to follow-up with another. Erasing each word letter by letter, like peeling the petals off a rose, she feels sorry for herself and wishes she hadn't been so naive.

Margaret strokes Penelope's head over the side of the tub as her thoughts spiral into a storm of self-pity. A whole new kind of lonely washes over her.

Maybe he was just telling me what I wanted to hear. Maybe he met someone else. Maybe he realized it was just too much work.

Her bath bomb has completely dissolved, and the water is now cool and sparkly. Margaret emerges from the tub. Toweling off, she observes her shriveled skin. The sight makes her feel even older and more pitiful than before.

Throwing on an oversized T-shirt and scooping up Penelope Grace, Margaret curls into bed. She turns on her comfort show and reaches for her journal to enter today's entry.

While it doesn't do her any good, she rereads the last few days' worth under the guise of "inspiration."

> *Feeling blah. Bored. Lonely. Sad. Still no word... Had a much-needed girls' night with Britt tonight. Pizza, wine, and a rom-com marathon. Thankful to have her as a local friend and great listener!*

> *Worked extra-long at work today because I didn't have anything better to do. Finally getting the hang of things and feel like I'm doing really well! Amanda had great things to say during our check-in today :)*

> *Feeling homesick. So excited to be going home soon for Thanksgiving. Was supposed to go on a trivia night date, but obviously, that didn't happen. Fingers crossed for next time...*

Instead of picking up her pen and embracing her emotions, Margaret snaps the book shut and shoves it back into the drawer it came from. In desperate need of a venting session, she calls her best friend instead.

"Hey, girl!" Tess says, chipper as always.

"Hey, are you busy?" Margaret asks with the call on speakerphone as she picks at her cuticles. "Did I catch you at a bad time? We can talk later…"

"Nope, of course not. I'm just doing the dishes, so it's a perfect time!" Margaret can hear the water whooshing and plates clanking together between words. "What's up with you? I feel like we haven't chatted in forever!"

Margaret considers her answer carefully, lying flat on her back and staring at the spinning fan overheard. "Ugh, honestly, so much has happened."

The water cuts off in the background. "Oh? What do you mean?" Tess asks, her tone a mixture of serious and concerned.

"Tess..." Margaret trails off, acknowledging her embarrassment and the fact that her friends were right.

"Talk to me," Tess says encouragingly.

Margaret exhales. "It's Hayes. I think you all might have been right."

She can hear Tess crumble on the other end of the line, her disappointment obvious. "Oh, sis, I'm so sorry. What's going on?"

Margaret spares her the details but tries to explain the situation to the best of her ability. "We had what I thought was a great conversation that night that he came for his confessional," Margaret huffs, attempting to diffuse her heartache with humor, "but then he just up and ghosted me. No word. No reason. No explanation. Nothing."

Anger and frustration creep into her voice, both her mind and heart crying out, "*Why?*"

"It's like he said what he knew I wanted to hear but didn't mean a word of it."

"Ugh, I wish I could say something to make it better. The only thing I know is he is a fool to let you go," Tess says matter-of-factly. "He will regret it one of these days."

Rolling over and propping herself up on her elbows, Margaret says, "I just hate the not knowing. It wasn't like I knew it was going to last forever, but I definitely didn't think it would end this way." Her lip quivers, but she refuses to let the tears fall.

On a mission to cheer herself up, Margaret tucks the phone into her bra strap and heads for the kitchen.

"I don't think this is about you. You didn't do anything wrong. You are amazing, and you better not forget it. One of these days, some guy is going to come along and recognize it right off the bat, okay?"

Everyone needs a friend like Tess.

Margaret retrieves the ice cream carton from the freezer and the toppings from the fridge and pantry. "I know, I know. But it doesn't make it any easier."

She scoops the leftover frozen candy bar goodness into a bowl as Tess continues her wise pep-talk.

"No, it doesn't. It's okay to feel all the feelings. Acknowledge them. Then move on whenever the time is right."

Margaret adds sprinkles, strawberries, and chocolate syrup. "I appreciate you. I should have seen this coming. You all tried to warn me… I can't believe how naive I was."

She is putting up the cold stuff when Tess says, "Sometimes love, or what we think is love, will blind us. It's nothing to be ashamed of. That's what we're here for!"

"Yeah," Margaret agrees, returning to her bed and a patient Penelope Grace. "Tess?" Margaret waits for her acknowledgment before saying, "Can we not tell the others? Or will you tell them for me? I don't want to talk about it any more than I have to."

"Absolutely. They will understand."

"You're the best ever, ever, ever," Margaret says between oversized bites of ice cream sundae.

Margaret shifts the topic of conversation to Tess, Ben, their new house, and their jobs.

"Work is keeping me busy for sure, but it's okay right now. Ben has made some sales recently, which is exciting, and he is really enjoying all the house projects. Me? Not so much."

The thought of Tess doing anything remotely messy, or home improvement related, makes Margaret laugh. "I can only imagine... I would pay to see you on a ladder!"

"Shut up!" Tess says playfully. "I just have to keep reminding myself that it will be worth it when it's done."

Margaret hears the sound of running water resume in the background, evidence Tess has returned to his dish washing and kitchen tidying duties.

"Speaking of, is there a timeline?"

"We're hoping sometime in the next month! Our goal is to have everything in a good place by the Christmas party, but no promises. It is still very much a work in progress, so don't get your hopes up."

"Totally understand. I kinda feel the same way about my place. I'm not sure the boxes will ever go away."

Once their laughs fizzle out, the girls say their goodbyes, and Tess offers some parting wisdom. "Don't beat yourself up over this, okay? It's his loss. Don't you forget it!"

Feeling exponentially better now than she did thirty minutes ago, Margaret gives her journal entry one more stab.

Self-care night with PG + broke the news about H to Tess. Couldn't ask for a better, more supportive friend. It's not me. It's him. The best is yet to come. <3

CHAPTER 17

———

Looking at himself in the mirror, Hayes positions a plain black tie around his neck and replays his dad's directions in his mind.

"*Across the front, up the neck, thru the loop, and tighten,*" he would say, constantly peering over Hayes's left shoulder.

While his father hasn't instructed him in at least fifteen years, the memory of his guidance brings comfort on this day in particular. Dressed in a basic black suit, now complete with a matching tie, Hayes prepares to say goodbye to his father for the last time.

Turns out, the headaches his father had casually mentioned a few times were the first symptoms of a sentinel brain bleed. Emma and Wes finally took him to the hospital a few weeks ago to get checked out, and that's when everything changed. The doctors had initially diagnosed it as a stroke, which resulted in emergency neurosurgery. His father's aneurysm was clipped by the best neurosurgeon in Chicago, and Hayes arrived to find his dad unconscious, with a partially shaved head and a four-inch scar.

Jim remained hospitalized for the following week in recovery. The family rotated in and out, spending quality time with him. Grateful the bleed had been caught, all were hopeful the patriarch would make a full recovery. Though they knew the road ahead would be long and grueling, they thought they were in the clear.

Until, in the middle of the night, Hayes received yet another dreadful phone call. His father had suffered another bleed, this one fatal.

In a matter of a week, his life came crumbling down. His strong, healthy, and independent father was gone. As a result, his already ill mother became visibly and emotionally frailer. Hayes, too, found himself weak and more reliant on his siblings than ever before.

As a distraction and coping mechanism, Hayes volunteered to coordinate a celebration of life event to honor his father. Friends, family, neighbors, coworkers, and people Hayes didn't even know came from far and wide to pay tribute to his father. From elaborate floral arrangements to a thoughtfully curated playlist and catered lunch, the gathering was perfect. As perfect as a heart-wrenching event can be.

Emma, Jim's wife of thirty-nine years, sat on the front pew in utter disbelief, struggling to wrap her mind around the fact her high school sweetheart was no longer with her. His arm had always been around her at all times. Hayes summoned every ounce of strength and courage he had to support his fragile mom.

His mother had never thought his father would be the one to go first. No one did. They only ever spoke of what *he* would do *without her.*

It became apparent rather quickly that his mother had little will to live without the love of her life. Despite being relatively stable for the last six months, her numbers began to fall. Her body, mind, and soul were finally giving in because without Dad, it seemed as if there was no reason to continue.

The following week was a blur for the whole Thompson family. While attempting to get her husband's affairs in order and grieve his sudden loss, his mother declined rapidly. Her broken heart couldn't take it anymore. Instead of responding positively to her daily cancer treatments, her body began to reject them.

Five days later, Hayes, Wes, and Sam buried their mother in the plot adjacent to their father, the dirt and flowers still fresh.

* * *

It's been over a month since Hayes received that dreadful phone call from Wes, one that he didn't know at the time would change his life forever. Now, sitting in a pub down the street from his house, Hayes chugs the last of his second beer and motions to the bartender for another. Eyeing Wes and Sam's mugs on either side, he calls out, "Make that three, Jerry!"

Unsure how to cope or continue with life given the utter chaos of the last few weeks, Hayes requested a three-month leave of absence from work. Shawn promised his promotion would be waiting for him upon his return, whenever that may be. He has also decided to stay in Chicago with his brothers while they take care of their childhood home and parents' estate.

Though they have no plans to sell it anytime soon, there is still much to be done and taken care of. Today, for example, they tackled cleaning out the contents of the garage and Dad's old toolshed. By the end of the chore, the brothers agreed their father's only fault was that he never threw a single thing away.

Proud of their progress and accomplishments, they decided to celebrate at Hannigan's, their old stomping grounds and a place their father loved to frequent with his golf buddies.

Sipping on his third pint of the evening, Hayes notices the lights dimming and bartenders gearing up in preparation for the evening crowd. Out of his peripherals, he sees a female of average height with shoulder-length brown hair, gesturing passionately as she tells a story to a small audience of bar patrons. The oddly familiar sight sends a wave of pain, sadness, regret, and loneliness crashing over him.

It isn't Margaret, of course.

But the thought of her makes him ache.

He cracks his knuckles and stretches out his neck in an effort to relieve the stress and tension that accompany the memory of her.

Hayes tries to recall their last conversation but struggles. He vaguely remembers exchanging a few texts in the days that followed his confession at her apartment, but the details are hazy.

When he lost his phone at the airport as part of the travel frenzy, his contacts had not been backed up since 2020. So not only was he phoneless but contactless, too. Overwhelmed with where even to begin or how to reach her, he chose to take the easy way out.

Silence.

Numb with guilt and regret, he opts to do nothing but let his pain fester.

She probably already moved on. I should have reached out. She deserves better. I bet she hates me.

Hannigan's, decked out with Irish decor and traditional stained-glass lighting, has an entirely different atmosphere than Fred's. Even still, it is familiar and homey, two things Hayes has longed for over the past few weeks.

Sitting on a well-broken-in leather barstool, Hayes eavesdrops on conversations around him, feeling both invisible and out of place.

Wes and Sam talk across him about everything from football to their wives and the remaining arrangements that need to be made. While the loss of their parents has taken a toll on them all, his brothers seem to be coping better. Having been close to their parents and on good terms all these years, it seems as though finding peace comes much easier for them.

"Did you see the game last night? That was a crazy catch in the fourth quarter!" Sam says, his eyes on the TV above them featuring replays and highlights.

"I didn't watch it live because I was dealing with the girls. But I caught the recap this morning... I racked up quite a few points!" Wes says with pride in reference to his fantasy team.

"How's your matchup looking this week?" Sam asks.

How can they talk about such trivial things?

Throwing back the rest of his drink, Hayes does his best to tune them out and shift his focus elsewhere.

Meanwhile, in a booth behind him, a female voice asks, "So, are you from the area?"

"Sorta... grew up outside of town, went to college, then moved to the city after graduation," her date shares.

Listening to their small talk, he cannot help but reflect on his first date with Margaret. Oh, how he was a completely different person back then—carefree yet career-focused. Leaving notes on napkins, packing elaborate picnics, and overthinking every text message he sent...

His posture weakens, and his head hangs. He fiddles with the condensation on the outside of his mug and the shriveled-up coaster Jerry tossed his way when he first sat down. The Hannigan's logo, once bold, prominent, and unmistakable, is now soggy and illegible. A perfect metaphor for himself.

While Hayes has always been more of a listener than a talker, his preference has shifted from participant to total observer. Unsure what to say or how to partake in casual conversations, he keeps to himself instead. He speaks only when spoken to, and sometimes not even then.

"Hayes?" Sam asks. "Did you hear me, dude?"

"Sorry, what?" Hayes scrambles.

Shaking his head, Sam asks, "Were you listening to any of that?" His fist falls on the bar top in exasperation.

With his lips pursed together, Hayes nods and tries to play off his total lack of attention to the conversation.

"We were just talking about what we're going to do tomorrow," Wes says, quickly recapping the consensus. "Clean up the landscaping and haul off the rest of the trash, at least."

Hayes is agreeable but doesn't contribute anything additional.

What did I do to deserve all of this?

Across the bar, he nods to Jerry with raised eyebrows, signing his desire for another. Their nonverbal communication is exactly what Hayes needs right now.

Observing the various groups around him, Hayes considers how disconnected from the world he feels. With no desire to do anything about it, he concludes perhaps he *deserves* to be alone. It's better for everyone this way.

The dark-haired woman to his left laughs again, sending a pang of agony and loneliness to his gut.

Jerry approaches Hayes with his refill in hand and whispers, "Have ya called her?"

Hayes snaps his head, making immediate eye contact with the jolly old man. Confused and stumbling over his words, he asks, "What? Who?" He looks around the bar for context clues, wondering if perhaps Jerry has mistaken him for someone else.

Jerry is probably in his late sixties, his hair gray and hands wrinkled. He's been here every time Hayes has stopped by, but they have never exchanged more than beer orders and cash.

"The girl," he says matter-of-factly before turning away and tending to used mugs in need of a wash. When he doesn't get a response, he repeats his first question again, this time more deliberately. "Have you called her?"

"Called *who*?" Hayes asks with a pinch of frustration in his voice, emphasizing *who* even more this time. He pushes the barstool a couple of inches farther away from the bar, addressing his need for more personal space. His movement catches the attention of Sam and Wes, meaning he now has six eyes watching his every move rather than just two.

Jerry chuckles, shaking his head at Hayes's obliviousness. "The girl you're thinking about. The one who broke your heart… or the one whose heart you broke, can't tell which yet." He speaks casually as if they are buddies. Like Hayes has confided in him about his relationship struggles.

Is this guy crazy?

"How did you know about that?" Hayes shifts in his seat, trying to understand what is happening and how Jerry knows about his love life. Or lack thereof. Glancing between the guys, he asks, "What did y'all tell him?"

Throwing their hands up in the air as if proclaiming their innocence, Wes says, "Don't look at me! I didn't do shit!"

"Me either. That's all you, buddy," Sam adds.

In unison, Wes and Sam take mischievous sips of their beers and nod at Jerry as if to say, *"Nice work. Keep it up."*

"Son, I've been a bartender for over half my life. I can spot a broken heart from a million miles away," Jerry says, scanning his bar crowd with pride. "Ya learn a lot by watchin' people. Just lookin' at their faces will tell ya 'bout anything you need to know."

"And what exactly is my face saying?" Hayes asks.

"That you're sad and alone but wish ya weren't," Jerry says with a casual shrug as if he's an expert on face reading.

Nodding ever so slightly, Hayes neither confirms nor denies Jerry's suspicions. Instead, he retreats to the restroom to plot his escape.

Sliding back up to the bar and taking a big gulp, his thoughts are interrupted by his new friend once more.

"I'm gonna take that as a no… You oughta call her. See if you can make up," his overly presumptuous bartender advises. "Don't wanna let a good one get away. They're hard to come by these days."

Hayes senses Jerry is speaking from experience. "I'm not sure she wants, uh…" Hayes hesitates, realizing he's not at all sure what Margaret wants, "to hear from me."

"Well, if ya don't know, ya oughta try. Got nothin' to lose."

Hayes leans back on the rickety barstool, contemplating Jerry's perspective. "Well, unfortunately, I don't even know how I would get in touch with her."

Eyeing him, Jerry keeps his thoughts to himself for the first time.

"Seriously? That's your excuse?" Wes asks, spinning his coaster on its edge like a coin.

"It's hardly an excuse. I don't know what I'd say, much less how I'd say it!" Hayes says defensively.

As he ponders the situation further, the brunette laughs *again*. The sound penetrates his mind and his heart, serving as an audible reminder of what *could be* but *isn't*.

"Regardless, I'm no good for her. She deserves better." Focusing on his beer, the carbonation bubbling inside the gradually defrosting glass, and the amber color amplified by the bar's lighting, he adds, "Prob'ly already moved on."

And I deserve to be alone.

"Bro, come on. You've got nothing to lose," Sam says. "You have to let the walls come down eventually."

"And if you need anything, if we can ever help you or you want to talk things through, just tell us," Wes offers. "We're here for you. Even when you aren't actually *here*."

Resting his elbows on the bar, Hayes shrugs off the advice despite knowing they're right. While he doesn't verbally acknowledge them, he does make a pledge to himself to try to be better. More open.

While he believes Margaret deserves better and it *is* possible she has already moved on, the truth is, he can't lose anyone else. He has experienced enough pain and loss in the past month to last a lifetime.

It's better this way.

Thwack! Jimmy's fist makes contact with the bar less than twelve inches from Hayes's head.

"Better get after her, or you're gonna miss your chance. Good women don't wait around long…" The way he raises his eyebrows reminds Hayes of his mom—her trademark way of saying, *"You better listen to me, or else."*

Interpreting this subtle reminder of his mom as the universe's way of telling him to stop making excuses, Hayes stands, pushing the barstool away from him with unintentional force, and throws a hundred-dollar bill down on the counter—for the beers and the discounted therapy session.

He quickly says goodbye to his brothers, promising to see them tomorrow for more manual labor. Then, on his way out the door, Hayes throws Jerry a casual salute—ending their friendship in the same nonverbal manner that it began.

CHAPTER 18

―――

"If I didn't know better, I would think you were taking a walk of shame," Amanda says, assessing Margaret's look of the day with her arms folded across her chest.

Tossing Amanda a dramatic eye roll, Margaret looks down at her attire and shrugs.

Having rolled out of bed far later than her alarm suggested, Margaret was forced to throw on the most convenient outfit possible—a wrinkled business casual dress she found on the floor of her closet. She put her hair in a clip without even running a brush through it and was out the door in a flash. Her mother would be appalled.

On the upside, she did manage to grab an actual matching pair of shoes! While this may not sound like anything worth celebrating, considering she strolled into the office with one brown and one black ballet flat yesterday, this is an improvement. Baby steps.

"Feeling any better today?" Amanda asks.

"A little," Margaret says without conviction, shuffling papers and setting up her workstation on autopilot.

"I'll take that as a no. What can I do to cheer you up?" Amanda asks, her hands folded together like a pleading child.

Though they were just casual coworkers at first, Amanda and Margaret have become fast friends over the last few months, spending more time together than with anyone else. Margaret has confided in Amanda regarding her relationship struggles and the emotional rollercoaster she has been on. In addition to the professional advice she's obligated to provide as Margaret's designated mentor, Amanda has also offered unconditional support and honest feedback too.

Margaret shrugs again, this time more apathetically. "I don't know. Maybe we could go to happy hour or something after work?"

Jumping up and down, Amanda gasps as if a light bulb has just turned on inside her brain. "Yes! I know the perfect place!"

While she doesn't reveal anything else, her excitement is contagious and gives Margaret something to look forward to as she cranks through client proposals and presentation prep.

Unsure where else to put her energy these past six weeks, Margaret has poured 110 percent of her effort into her job. And, aside from today, she's established a routine of arriving early and staying late. She's been intentional in building relationships with both her coworkers and clients, their friendship and advice instrumental in her professional development.

The lack of distracting texts and fewer extended "working lunches" have allowed her to focus exclusively on her projects, progressing quickly and earning praise along the way. Her list of responsibilities is multiplying, and her work ethic was recently described as "impressive" by Lacey.

Success.

Amanda rounds the corner with her bag slung over her shoulder and lip gloss recently reapplied just as Margaret shuts down for the day. Amanda's smile, a perfect contender for a Crest commercial, is accentuated by subtle pink sparkles and is on full display this afternoon.

"No more work for today, ma'am. Let's get outta here!" Amanda says, shaking a finger in the air as if to say *tsk tsk* and proactively prohibit any protests.

"You'll be pleased to know I was just packing up. I'm ready," Margaret says, sliding her laptop into her chic work bag and trading in her "work slippers" for the *matching* mules beneath her desk.

At Lush-ous, Amanda's new hidden gem for postwork cocktails, the girls rehash drama from earlier in the week with their other team members. Margaret peppers her with questions related to their clients, team, and office politics, still trying to get up to speed on the ins and outs of everything.

With all the work talk out of the way, they are left with only the elephant in the room to discuss. The latest, or lack thereof, with *Mr. Americano.*

Margaret swirls the last few sips of her Lemon Drop, forcing Amanda to initiate.

"So," Amanda begins, attempting to chip away at the ice rather than shatter it right off the bat.

Margaret looks up, knowing what's coming next but not giving her the satisfaction of divulging quite so quickly. "Yesssss?" she asks slowly, her legs beginning to bounce nervously.

"Have you heard *anything* from him?" Amanda's tone is hopefully optimistic. "Anything at all?"

"Nope." Margaret pops her lips together for added emphasis and takes a sip. "Nothing."

By now, the modern cocktail bar and tapas restaurant has filled in. All barstools are occupied, and plenty of patrons are standing around, waiting for the opportunity to view the menu and place their orders. The music has been cranked up a notch, taking the vibe from quiet and intimate to more casual and conversational. The change in volume puts Margaret at ease, diminishing her concern about someone eavesdropping on her embarrassing situation.

"Okay, not to sound stalkerish or anything," Amanda prefaces, "but I may have taken to social media…" She pauses to gauge Margaret's reaction.

"And?" Margaret maintains an even-keeled tone, unsure what she's about to learn.

"Well, we already knew all he has is an outdated Facebook page…"

"Right," Margaret confirms, thinking this is old news considering they have been down this path too many times to count.

"Still nothing there. Unfortunately." Amanda momentarily displays a pouty frown and dramatic slouch before exposing the rest of her truth. "But, through some sneaky backend investigation, I think I was able to find his brothers' accounts…"

Margaret tilts her head with interest and says, "Do tell," over the rim of her coupe glass.

"It took some doing and reverse searching, but yes. I found Wes first, then Sam. Both of their accounts are überprivate, so I can't see anything besides their profile pictures."

Her hope of a promising lead or explanation fizzles out. "Oh," Margaret says. "That's a bummer."

"Yeah, I know," Amanda agrees, reaching for her phone to pull up said accounts for Margaret to study. "I mean, if worse comes to worst, you could always reach out to one of them if you need to…"

At Amanda's words, Margaret gets a sinking feeling in her stomach. "What if something is wrong? What if he's not just ghosting me?"

It isn't the first time that she has had these thoughts, but it *is* the first time she has vocalized them.

What if?

Amanda hands over her phone with Facebook open and Wes's account on display. His profile picture was updated earlier this month to a childhood photo of what appears to be him and his parents. Margaret scrolls through the account, unable to view much else, before swiping over to Sam's, which features some odd similarities.

"They both changed their profile pictures recently," Margaret observes. "Like really recently." She flips back and forth to compare. "And they both have photos with their parents now," she adds, attempting to decipher what this means.

Amanda nods. "I kind of noticed that too…"

"I don't know what to make of this," Margaret says, shaking her head and returning the phone to Amanda. "But it really makes me wonder if there's something else, something bigger, going on here."

"I mean, it's possible…" Amanda's skeptical tone, pursed lips, and squinted eyes say otherwise, though.

Noted.

Amanda squeezes Margaret's knee in solidarity. "Listen, regardless of what happened and his reasons, you deserve better. Life's too short to wait around for texts from silly boys. Okay?"

While her facial expression remains downturned, Margaret nods in affirmation, still seeking to add meaning to the throwback photos.

"We will find you the perfect guy. Or at least one to get your mind off Mr. Americano…"

"Damn americanos. I can hardly drink them anymore!" Margaret teases, throwing back the rest of her drink.

"I have an even better idea," Amanda says, motioning for the bartender to head their way. "Two Espresso Martinis, please," she requests, her perfect white teeth on display yet again.

"Talk to me about your ideal guy," Amanda instructs, the gears evidently turning inside her brain.

Margaret attempts to describe her dream man, but every characteristic that comes to mind pertains to Hayes.

Tall. Sharp and smart looking. Can pull off a casual button-down. Funny and cultured.

Her judgment clouded and prohibiting her from providing an unbiased list of criteria, Margaret claims she doesn't have a type.

"But *everyone* has a type," Amanda challenges, proceeding to describe her own.

For the rest of the evening, Amanda resorts to pointing out potential men for Margaret and gauging her interest that way.

"He looks too old for me," Margaret says about a man sitting alone on the other side of the bar with salt and pepper hair.

"I'm not really into redheads. I'm not totally opposed, just not my preference…" she says about another, making Amanda chuckle.

When she points to a guy at the front of the bar sporting a loosened tie and slightly unbuttoned dress shirt, Margaret's face lights up, and her cheeks warm. "He's h-handsome," she stutters with stars in her eyes. Smiling, she admires his build and perfect posture before noticing the ring on his left hand and deflating.

"Ugh!" Amanda says, noting the silver band on his ring finger. "This is helpful, though. I know what I'm looking for now, and I will start my search right away!"

"You're hilarious," Margaret says sarcastically. "I'm not sure I'm ready for that, but I know I need to move on. It's time."

They share a few more laughs before parting ways. While the conversation and drinks at Lush-ous were relaxing, the quality girl time only served as a band-aid for Margaret's pain and heartache.

As soon as she is alone, the loneliness threatens to creep in as her own words echo in her mind.

I need to move on. I need to move on. I need to move on.

An impossible directive given the state of her broken heart and confused mind.

When she gets home, Margaret pulls out her journal to put her commitment in writing.

Great night at Lush-ous! Yummy drinks, good vibes, great convo.
Officially decided that today is the day I'm committing to moving on.
I will not think about Mr. Americano anymore. —MP

She initials the entry to make the promise real.
No more Mr. Americano.

CHAPTER 19

"I'm hurrying!" Margaret says, frantically answering Britt's call without even giving her a chance to speak.

"You better be!" Britt says, exasperated. "See you out front in a min!"

Living out her pledge of *no more Mr. Americano*, Margaret has said yes to more events and activities in the last couple of weeks than she ever has before. Despite her best efforts, she hasn't been on time for one of them, which has become a source of tension with Britt, her most Type A friend. Margaret has added punctuality to her list of upcoming new year's resolutions.

Tonight, the girls are going to a tacky Christmas sweater party at Fred's with a collection of Britt's friends, including a few guys she claims are a "perfect fit" for Margaret.

Margaret spent all afternoon decorating her sweater for the event to ensure she made the best impression possible. Her cream turtleneck with a sequin stocking sewn on the front is equal parts tacky and cute. The stocking holds an entire bottle of white wine, and the words *My Kind of White Christmas* are scribbled on an attached tag. *Clever.*

Margaret evaluates her look consisting of her homemade sweater, black leather leggings that hug her in all the right places, and tinsel in her hair. She does a little spin, verifying everything is up to par.

"Fabulous if I do say so myself!"

Knowing Britt is likely pacing anxiously along the sidewalk, glancing at the clock every five seconds, and panicking they'll be late, Margaret spastically shuffles through the heap of shoes on the floor. Despite her closet looking like a war zone, *again*, she manages to locate a pair of chunky black booties. Achieving cute, casual, and comfy, she makes a mad dash for the door.

"Finally!" Britt calls out, looking at her watchless wrist, just as Margaret expected. "I was beginning to think you were going to stand me up!"

"Oh, shut up," Margaret says, reaching for a quick hug. "You know I've been looking forward to this for weeks!"

The girls slip into their perfectly timed ride-share as Britt says, "Of course, and I totally love how your sweater turned out! Even better than the inspo pic!"

Shimmying, Margaret shows off her bedazzled masterpiece, pleased with her craft skills. "Why thank you, I think it's pretty wine-derful if I must say so myself!"

The pun earns her an eye roll from Britt before she quickly changes the subject. "So, I feel like I haven't seen you in ages! What's new? How was your Thanksgiving?"

Margaret tells her about her trip home and the extended family time. "It was pretty low-key. I feel like all we did was cook and eat the whole time," Margaret exaggerates. "My mom and I spent practically every waking moment together, which was great, but also, a little bit of her goes a long way," she says with a wink.

"If it makes you feel any better, same for me," Britt says. "My sister had drama, per usual. I think my mom baked at least a dozen pies as a coping mechanism due to said drama. Then, on top of that, I had to answer the usual slew of adulting questions about my work and love life, or lack thereof. You know the drill."

"Oh, do I," Margaret says with frustration. "All weekend long, my mom was fishing for information. Bless her heart, she tries to be sneaky, but she just doesn't have it in her."

Britt empathizes, sharing similar stories about her own mother's quest for details. "I know she means well, but my lack of a relationship is literally the *last thing* I want to talk about with her!"

As they pull up in front of Fred's, Britt says, "Just to clarify. You haven't heard from *him*, have you?"

Silent Night? More like Silent Month…

Shooting her a sharp look, Margaret lets her silence speak for itself. She pretends to zip her lips and throw away the key.

"Good, I think that's for the best. I have someone else in mind for you anyway." She weaves her arm through Margaret's and guides them through the festive red and green sea.

Christmas lights are hung overhead, and various holiday songs serve as background noise. Ripped tissue paper litters the floor, and half-opened presents sit on top of tables while givers and receivers mingle. Though there are many tacky sweaters in sight, they all pale in comparison to Margaret's original piece of art.

Britt, being the social butterfly she is, introduces Margaret to everyone in the crew. Margaret does her best to channel her inner Britt, putting on her conversationalist hat, batting her eyelashes and all.

Throughout the evening, Margaret attempts to flirt with various guys, all of whom Britt introduces her to. Her charm wins her numerous seasonal beverages, countless belly laughs, and two new contacts in her phone. With her mantra of *I need to move on* pulsating in her brain, Margaret decides to let loose and go wherever the night takes her—including the arms of a personal trainer named Alex.

His knack for storytelling—smooth, sarcastically humorous, and not overly rehearsed—caught her ear from afar. She had been standing on the opposite side of the group near Britt at the time but eventually summoned the courage to break away and make her own moves.

By midnight, she can't peel her eyes off his lips or pry her hands from his arms. Though Alex doesn't fit the mold for her typical "type," as determined by Amanda the other night at Lush-ous, he's here, seems nice enough, and is paying her attention.

What more do I need?

They sneak out the back to a bench along the river. Margaret attempts to drown out the flood of memories she has here with *him*, but she can't. All the while, her lips are pressed against Alex's, the logical and emotional sides of her brain are at war.

> *I wish Hayes was here.*
> > *No, you don't.*
> *He's so great.*
> > *He hurt you.*
> *I miss kissing him.*
> > *He's probably kissing someone else.*

When the floodlights are flicked on at last call, the mood shifts and Margaret comes to her senses. She peels herself off Alex and uses Britt as an excuse to break away. "I'm sorry, my friend says it's time to go…"

"You don't have to leave if you don't want to," he says, glancing over his shoulder with a sexy smile smeared across his face.

"It's probably for the best. I need to check on my dog anyway." Margaret gives him a quick peck on the cheek and thanks him again for a fun evening.

"You bet. Let's do it again sometime." The corner of his mouth curves upward just as he turns and walks off.

Back with Britt, she confesses all the details of her escapade. While her rosy cheeks and swollen lips are a dead giveaway as to what *happened,* they don't reveal anything about how she *felt.*

"I got what I thought I wanted, but apparently, it wasn't what I needed," Margaret says, defeated. "The whole time we were making out, I just kept wishing it was *him,* and I hate myself for it!"

"Oh, honey," Britt says, giving Margaret a gentle side hug. "Don't beat yourself up over it. It's okay. It happens to the best of us," she adds, almost dismissively.

"I know it's okay, but he doesn't deserve that kind of space in my brain! I just want to forget about him and how damn good of a kisser he is!"

Back at Margaret's apartment but not ready to call it quits for the evening, Britt helps her curate the perfect online dating persona. They work to select the best photos and prompts to portray Margaret as the ambitious, adventure-loving dog mom she is.

Within minutes, she is getting matches and date inquiries, both of which are just the ego boost she needed this evening.

"Thanks for your help, Britt," Margaret says as she walks her friend to the door. "I'll let you know if any of these guys are promising."

Bouncing up and down on her tiptoes, arguably more invested in the outcome than Margaret, Britt says, "Yes, you *must* keep me posted! I want all the deets!"

Leading up to Christmas, Margaret goes on a few casual dates here and there, none of which show great potential. However, after each date, Margaret feels less and less inclined to keep trying. Not because she's giving up but because she finally feels *content*.

Rather than looking to someone else to satisfy her needs and contribute to her happiness, Margaret looks inward.

This weekend, she and her college besties are gathering for their annual Christmas party, one of Margaret's favorite weekends of the year! While the thought of reliving the last month's pain just so they are "up to speed" once made her quiver, it now hardly makes her bat an eye.

Earlier this week, Tess texted asking everyone for a head count and ETA. Though it generally pains Margaret to say she'll be coming alone, this time, she feels relieved. No one to tend to, take care of, or include in small talk. A blessing.

The last to arrive at the festivities, per usual, Margaret is excited and anxious to catch up with her friends.

Knock, knock, knock.

"Merry Christmas, sista!" Tess cheers, swinging the front door of her new house with great enthusiasm. "Come in, come in! Let me grab that from you," she says, reaching for the tray of homemade pinwheel wraps from Margaret and ushering her inside.

Caroline, Susannah, and their husbands make a receiving line to greet Margaret, each offering a hug and friendly smile. "I'm so glad to finally be here!" Margaret says, acknowledging everyone and taking in the jolly scene.

The living area, complete with an oversized Christmas tree, holiday-themed decorative pillows, carols playing in the background, and the scent of freshly baked cookies in the air, is comfortable and homey. Margaret spreads her various potluck contributions on the dining table, peppering her friends with questions and compliments every chance she gets.

While Margaret never followed up on what exactly Tess told the others, she trusts she provided a fair and comprehensive update. Neither Caroline nor Susannah ever mention he-who-shall-not-be-named or say, "I told you so," even though they have every right.

The best kinds of friends.

At dinner, the couples sit across from one another, and Margaret proudly serves as the head of the table. While this, too, used to make her self-conscious, tonight she chooses to embrace it, her position allowing her to play an equal part in every conversation.

Afterward, the clan relocates to the backyard for a bonfire. As Tess complains of Ben's snoring, Caroline wishes Logan knew how to sleep in, and Susannah can't get comfortable as a result of the tiny human growing inside of her, Margaret chooses to find the bright side in her singleness... Only one calendar to worry about, the whole bed to herself, less responsibility, more freedom... The list could go on and on.

None of the girls outright ask about Mr. Americano because they know Margaret well enough to know she will bring him up if she wants to. They do, however, inquire if she's been on any *other dates*. Margaret admits to her dating app usage, proudly showing off her meticulously crafted profile without revealing too much else.

But snuggled under flannel blankets and sipping on spiked hot chocolate, Margaret shrugs and gives in. "Okay, okay. I've matched with a few guys…"

Ooh-ing and ahh-ing commence from her audience.

She gives them their moment before continuing. "And I have even been on a few dates…"

Further excitement erupts from those in earshot.

"Don't get too carried away now. I'm happy where I am and with how things are going. I feel like the right guy will come along at the right time," Margaret says, now unsure whether she's trying to convince herself or her friends.

"Amen! That's what happened for me with Logan," says Caroline, glancing at her new hubby and twisting the stunning solitaire on her ring finger.

"Always happens when you're least expecting it," Tess confirms, blushing at the sight of her man putting more logs on the fire.

While the others laugh and continue chitchatting on the side, Susannah leans in and probes deeper. "I totally agree with you. But I just want to make sure you're okay…" Susannah trails off, reaching for Margaret's hands and looking her in the eye.

Margaret shifts her gaze to the starry night sky, trying to find the words to articulate how she feels. Quieter and more uneasy than before, Margaret says, "I really am more content than I have ever been. But I think, deep down, it has a lot to do with not wanting to get hurt again."

Susannah scoots even closer. "I know, I know. It's not easy. But trust me," she says, squeezing Margaret's hand to the point of it almost turning blue, "the best is yet to come."

Margaret reaches up, her fingers curled into the sleeve of her shirt, to dab her eyes. She tilts her head back, hoping gravity will be on her side and reel the tears back in.

Maybe I'm not as content as I thought.

Susannah, always looking to lighten the mood, says, "Maybe you just have to kiss a few frogs before you find your prince."

Margaret wraps her into a hug and whispers in her ear, "You're going to be the *best* girl mom, Sus. Thank you."

Maybe you just have to kiss a few frogs before you find your prince.

Margaret repeats the words to herself, wanting to remember them for her journal entry later on and smiling at the fact that Susannah called Hayes a frog.

CHAPTER 20

The first holiday season without Hayes's parents was rough.

Thanksgiving came around before reality even had a chance to set in. Though Hayes's sisters-in-law prepared all the traditional dishes and his nieces were responsible for the placemats like normal, it was most definitely *not* normal. The glue that held them together was missing. There were two empty seats at the table that no one was prepared for.

By Christmas, Hayes was no longer numb to the pain; the once *completely* open wound was at least starting to scab over. He embraced his role of Uncle H, filling the void in his life with the love of three little girls who absolutely adore him. Hayes and his brothers agreed not to force any traditions that were too painful or no longer felt like a fit. Instead, they built new habits together, something they all knew their mother would be thrilled about.

While New Year's Eve is not a holiday Hayes ever spent with his parents, it proved to be emotional, nonetheless. He watched college football all day and was in bed by 10 p.m., willing himself to think about anything *besides* Margaret. He assumed she was dancing the night away, rocking a short sequin dress, and kissing someone else.

Damn.

The thought of her alone, much less with someone else, remains a source of pain for Hayes. Even still, he can't seem to muster the courage to reach out, the fear of losing anyone else too much to bear. Though it's been close to two months since they have been together, her features are still ingrained in his mind.

In the last few months, he has wrestled with guilt, regret, and old trauma. Blaming himself for all the bad things that have gone wrong, including his dad's aneurysm and mother's cancer, despite both being completely out of his control.

While he has always thought of himself as a fixer, Hayes is experiencing a weird paradox where he, the fixer, is broken. Life has thrown rock after rock at him, chipping away at his hard exterior and stone-cold wall, making him fragile and emotional, falling victim to every lie and negative thought he tells himself.

With the new year underway, Hayes decides it's finally time to give Shawn another call. Their last conversation was brief and over email during the eye of the hurricane that wrecked his life. Hayes shared the logistics of his leave while Shawn expressed his understanding and condolences. They agreed to connect in January on the outstanding details.

So, with the new year underway, Hayes decides it's time to pick up the phone.

Walking along the pond behind his parents' house, his favorite thinking spot since his teen years, Hayes listens to the birds chirping and leaves rustling in the distance between rings.

"Hey, man! How are you?" Shawn asks.

"I'm making it," Hayes says honestly, skipping a rock across the pond. "And yourself? How are things going?"

"No complaints here! It's so good to hear from you, bud. We sure have missed ya," Shawn says after reemphasizing his heartfelt condolences to Hayes and the family.

Hayes continues his stroll along the water, kicking the occasional pine cone. "Likewise. Excited to get back into the swing of things."

"Still planning on coming back? Whew! That's good to hear!" Shawn says with exaggerated relief and a chuckle.

"Couldn't imagine doing anything else," Hayes assures him, having never considered any alternatives. "I was just calling to let you know I think I'm almost ready."

Hayes can hear the rest of the team celebrating in the background—a joyful sound he didn't realize how much he missed.

"Absolutely! We'll be ready whenever you are," his boss says, the background noise fizzling out as if he's just split off from the others. "How does February 1st sound to you? Is that enough time to get readjusted?" he asks, his genuine concern evident.

"Sounds great to me. Exactly what I had in mind," Hayes agrees, thinking that gives him about three more weeks to get things in order.

"Great. There is one thing we didn't get to talk about before... Regarding your promotion..." Shawn's tone shifts, more serious and calculated than before.

Halting in his tracks, Hayes can feel the tension building inside. *I can't take any more surprises.* He clears his throat in preparation for what is to come. "Yes?"

"This role in particular," Shawn pauses as if he's a game show host about to reveal what's behind curtain number one, "Is stationary. You will be permanently assigned to San Antonio."

San Antonio.

The sound of the word *permanent* almost makes his heart stop. While he was expecting an assignment eventually, he didn't think it would come so soon. And he *definitely* didn't think it would be in San Antonio.

The birds continue to chirp, and the leaves continue to rustle, but Hayes does not move or speak.

"Hayes? Is that going to be a problem for you?" Shawn asks, anxiety creeping into his voice.

"S-sorry," Hayes stammers. "Just processing... I must say, that's not exactly what I expected you to say."

"Understandably so. We don't typically make these decisions so quickly. But if you're comfortable with it, the team really needs you here in San Antonio."

San Antonio.

Margaret.

"Y-y-yeah, that sounds great, actually," Hayes says, resuming his walk along the bank and peering at his reflection in the water. "San Antonio is the only place I want to be."

Exactly what he didn't even know he wanted.

Hayes runs his hands through his hair, already thinking ahead and brainstorming his next move, both literally and figuratively.

He wraps up the conversation with Shawn and sends his salutations to the others in the office just as he approaches his parents' special spot.

They were both born and raised outside of Chicago and never experienced life anywhere else, but they always had each other, and this was always their home. For their first wedding anniversary, his dad built his mom a bench out of wood from the property. It's been here ever since.

It's weathered many a storm during its thirty-nine years of life. Perched on the edge, Hayes runs his fingers over the initials he carved into the arm during elementary school. He finds the W and L enclosed with a heart that Wes and Lara etched the day they got engaged at this exact spot, too.

With the thought of Texas on his mind, Hayes imagines where he will put his bench one day. And whose initials he'll carve next to his own.

SIX WEEKS LATER

Giddy, Hayes approaches the main entrance of his new home with shiny new keys clenched tightly in his hand. His palms are sweating despite the January air, and he fumbles a few times before successfully unlocking the door and stepping inside. Taking in the modern finishes and fresh paint smell, he is overcome with emotion.

It's even more stunning in person.

He paces around the open-concept floor plan and admires the kitchen, the main reason he bought the house. He runs his fingers along the cold marble countertops and brass hardware. Smiling with pride, Hayes is *happy* and at *home* for the first time in months.

He bought the house before seeing it in person. Crunched for time and convinced it was exactly what he was looking for, he put in a blind offer and hoped for the best.

Fortunately, the best is better than he could've ever imagined.

Over the following days, Hayes unpacks the few boxes that *actually* made the trip from Chicago and began to reestablish his old habits. Morning workouts at his favorite local gym, frequent grocery store runs to Central Market and the occasional stop by The Brew.

Today, he breaks away from his homeowner duties and the lingering paint fumes for a walk along the river.

Driving downtown, he thinks of his parents and how much he wishes they were here to witness this stage of his life. Despite their absence, he can feel their pride and knows they have the best view of anyone. Taking his exit, he observes a rainbow in the distance, arching behind the Alamodome, their subtle way of proving just that.

The January weather is pleasant, chilly enough to warrant a jacket, but nothing compared to the Windy City. Though he slipped his headphones into his pocket before leaving the house, Hayes decided to enjoy the scenery and sounds of nature instead. The hum of traffic in the distance, water lapping up against the rocks, and the buzz of other river walkers give him plenty to think about.

In front of him, women walk and talk while pushing strollers and wrangling wild children.

"Watch out, Max! Stay on the right side of the sidewalk," one of them yells as a biker comes zipping by, unfazed by Max's presence in the bike lane.

Off to the side, a young couple sits on wooden stumps, appearing to have a serious conversation. They face each other, eyes locked and hands intertwined in a heap. He plays out their story in his mind, assuming high school sweethearts talking about what life after graduation will entail.

Then, in the river, a group of tourists floats by, listening to slightly embellished history lessons and vying for complimentary T-shirts. "Remember the Alamo!" they cheer in unison as the guide gives them their cue.

Before he realizes it, Hayes has lost track of time and walked a few miles, the change in the pavement from concrete to gravel his primary indicator. Less familiar with this end of the river, he finds an oversized rock and uses it as an observation deck, taking in the view from all directions. Not quite ready to begin his trek back, he decides to treat himself to a little afternoon pick-me-up.

For convenience's sake, Hayes strides into the coffeeshop situated on the first floor of The Bella Hotel rather than making the trek to The Brew.

The vibe is similar. The scent of freshly ground coffee beans permeates the air, neutral colors cover the walls, and baristas buzz around in a frenzy.

But it is also foreign. More luxurious, less casual. The music is softer. The crowd is more mature. The barista is not Lucy, and, most notably, Margaret is not waiting for him at their corner table.

Hayes is pulled from his trance by the sound of the barista's voice. "Sir, what can I get for you today?"

Based on her impatient facial expression and drumming fingertips, he presumes that wasn't the first time she asked.

"Hi, sorry about that. Can I just get an iced americano?"

Scribbling on the side of a cup and without making eye contact, she says, "Yep, anything else?"

Hayes takes in the assortment of freshly baked pastries in the case. Strudels, kolaches, egg bites, mini muffins, and more are placed with perfect precision. He weighs his options before settling on a set of three mini cinnamon sugar muffins, his mouth watering in anticipation.

Every seat in the coffee shop is occupied, so Hayes finds a spot to prop himself against the wall. Staring off into space, oblivious to his surroundings, his mind hops from home projects to the weather to his readjustment at work.

Nearby, a feminine voice says, "Iced americano."

Assuming his order is ready, Hayes straightens and strides forward.

But rather than his cue for pickup, those two words signal a second chance.

CHAPTER 21

Margaret stands at the counter, completing her transaction for an iced americano and a trio of mini muffins.

"You got it! Those are popular today," the barista says, eyeing the bakery display and making Margaret feel even better about her choice.

As she steps away to get her belongings in order, an eerie feeling creeps in. Shifting her weight from one foot to the other and tucking her hair behind her ear, Margaret attempts to dissuade anyone from looking at her.

"Iced americano, ready at the bar!" one of the baristas calls out for all to hear. Looking up, Margaret makes a move but stops in her tracks as if she is in the middle of a game of freeze tag.

While part of her wishes he was only a figment of her imagination, the other part is over the moon to be in the same place as him again. Her heart begins to race, and her hands shake as if she has already consumed a double dose of caffeine on an empty stomach.

She's envisioned this moment more times than she can count. Thought about what she would do, how she would act, and what she might say. But none of those what-if scenarios prepared her for this moment. After retrieving his drink and side of cinnamon sugar muffins, he heads in her direction.

Of course, he ordered the damn muffins too.

The closer he gets, the slower his pace. His hair is longer now, shaggier than before, and stubble trails his jawline. His eyes, as piercingly blue as ever, are framed with dark circles, making him appear older and weathered. His proximity sends a shiver down her spine and causes goose bumps to populate on her skin.

"Hi," he says shyly, like a kid on the first day of kindergarten, fidgeting nervously and avoiding eye contact.

His meek and mild demeanor is a stark contrast to their first coffee shop encounter. Rather than confidence teetering on the edge of arrogance, he comes across as sensitive and fragile.

Catching a glimpse of her coffee and pastries over his shoulder, she nods and sidesteps him. Despite the techno music echoing through the small coffee shop, Margaret can only hear her pounding heart.

Nervousness, hope, anger, fear, and excitement fight for her mental capacity.

Get your shit together, she thinks, trying to act quickly.

Taking a deep breath, Margaret retraces her steps, struck again by his change in appearance.

"Hi," she finally manages, her cheeks warming and nerves multiplying by the second.

They stand in the middle of the coffee shop, still and silent, forcing others to weave around them like obstacles in the middle of the road. On the one hand, it feels as though all eyes are on them, and on the other, it feels like they are invisible to the world. Margaret grapples with which she prefers, both making her queasy and self-conscious.

Hayes breaks the awkward silence, his tone tentative. "Should we go somewhere else? Less crowded?"

Margaret nods and follows him, her mind void of conscious thoughts, consisting of only fragmented ideas and emotions. She recalls various journal entries she has made over the last few months, hoping they might inform how she should broach the conversation that is sure to come.

They follow the narrow pathway toward the river, just like on their first date. Suppressing the distant memories, Margaret reminds herself to focus on the present.

Though they are in the heart of the city, the world around them feels still. She hears the crunching of gravel beneath their feet, her own heavy breathing, and the thoughts inside her head, but nothing else.

Her senses heightened by his company, Margaret notices how the breeze feels chillier than before. She wishes she'd grabbed a jacket on the way out or at least a less-revealing sweater.

Her pulse quickens at Hayes's abrupt stop near a bench on the riverside.

Margaret sits down first, forcing him to make the call on how much distance to put between them, a game they seem to play every chance they get. Margaret recalls the rush of adrenaline she experiences when their fingers graze or their knees bump. The memory, combined with her desire for physical touch, has her wishing she had plopped down a few inches closer.

Orienting himself on the other end of the bench, Hayes clears his throat.

Oh god, here we go.

Margaret sits up a little straighter and messes with the cutout on her leggings, one of many purchases from a recent retail therapy session.

"I gotta say, I wasn't expecting to bump into you here... I thought you were loyal to Lucy and Lucy only?" His humor and the uptick at the edge of his mouth make her stomach flip-flop.

She messes with her hair and looks away, buying time to decide how playful she should be. "Lucy is by far the best, there's no doubt about that, but I've decided to branch out a little here and there," Margaret says without divulging any other details like *I can't go there without thinking about you, dumbass.*

Hayes nods with squinty eyes, suggesting he knows there's more to the story. As he opens his mouth to speak, Margaret takes control of the conversation.

"So..." Taking another sip of her coffee and reflecting on Caroline's advice during her intervention, she asks, "How have you been?" Concerned that may be too vague to solicit the information she's looking for, she tacks on, "What have you been up to? It's been quite a while..."

She avoids eye contact by admiring the steady flow of walkers, runners, and bikers on the path. Her knee was bouncing up and down unconsciously. Margaret waits for a stream of reasons and excuses to flow from his irresistible mouth.

Meanwhile, Hayes puts his arm along the back of their wooden bench, making Margaret acutely aware of his closeness. He looks down the river in the direction opposite her, his brow knit, and lips pursed together.

While the extended period of silence makes her uncomfortable, she's over being entangled in his web of lies and deception. She waits, reminding herself *he* is the one with explaining to do.

Slowly shifting his gaze back to her, Hayes says, "That's sort of a loaded question."

Oh, please. Rolling her eyes and crossing her arms, Margaret waits silently.

"So, before I explain all of that," he says gingerly, "I just want to apologize to you…"

Margaret tilts her head to the side like Penelope Grace does when she doesn't quite understand the command or wants someone's undivided attention.

"For everything. That I didn't tell you about the whole Chicago thing sooner, for leaving you without any warning, for all the times I stood you up, for not reaching out…" He trails off knowingly.

As he lists out his various offenses, Margaret is struck by how his voice mirrors his new posture and appearance. Vulnerable. Less confident. Hurt.

"I can only imagine how much I hurt you. And I want you to know I'm so, so sorry, Margaret," he continues, pleading for her forgiveness. When she *still* doesn't look his way, he gently brushes the hair off her shoulder, sending a jolt of electricity through her body.

"I just don't understand," she says, her voice shaky, eyes glassy, and tear ducts working overtime.

"You couldn't. I kept you in the dark and out of the loop. But now I want to tell you everything."

Confused, she says, "But I thought you already did?"

His hanging head says otherwise, and a pit forms in her stomach.

"You just disappeared, and it hurt." Her guard crumbling down and the pain resurfacing, she adds, "It hurt like hell, Hayes."

When she looks up, a single tear has fallen, leaving a trail of moisture from her eye to her jaw.

"I know. And, again, I can't tell you how sorry I am. I promise I can explain if you'll just let me."

"I'm sure you can…" Margaret says, fiddling with her paper straw, knowing she'll regret it later when she's slurping up cardboard. Her eyes finally meet his. "But we've already been through this once. I don't know that I can do it again."

CHAPTER 22

Margaret's eyes glisten in the sun as a few more tears fall.

It strikes Hayes that she is as broken as he is.

The only difference? Her pain is the direct result of *his* actions.

"Margaret..." he says, grasping for her attention as she walks away. "Please."

She doesn't stop or look over her shoulder at his plea. Instead, she continues down the paved path at a leisurely pace, occasionally glancing at the foliage off to one side or the other. Once she reaches the end of the sidewalk, she pivots and retraces her steps, looking everywhere but *at* him.

She sits, her back straight as a board and feet crossed at the ankle. Hayes notices her tears have dried, and her expression is stone-cold. She remains statue-like.

He cracks his knuckles and imagines his mother reprimanding him. He inhales sharply, preparing to come clean. For real, this time.

"Margaret, please let me explain."

She fumbles with her keychain, and her jaw is clenched tight.

"I'm sor—"

Bzz. Bzz. Bzz.

Hayes is cut off by the vibrating of her phone.

This feels familiar. He flashes back to the first time he ever tried to speak to her.

As Margaret sneaks a peek at the caller ID, the color disappears from her face. "I've got to take this," she whispers.

She stands abruptly and strides away again, this time with more purpose and *not* because of him.

Hayes observes her mannerisms, spastic and concerned. Almost out of earshot, all he can make out is her saying, "Are you sure she's going to be okay?" A few beats pass before Margaret clarifies again, "You're sure? All right. I'll be right there."

She ends the call and slips the phone into her pocket, panic painted across her face.

"It's Penelope," she says, breathy. "I need to go."

Trying to cover up his disappointment and knowing her pain all too well, he says, "Completely understand. Is everything okay?"

"She was in an accident with one of the bigger dogs at day camp. I'm not sure what happened or how serious it is, but I need to meet her at the animal hospital right away," she explains, her maternal instincts kicking in despite the tears welling in her eyes.

Hayes nods and stands to give her a quick hug. Even after the months they spent apart, he can't help but acknowledge how perfectly they still fit together.

Squashing his selfish observations, he says, "I hope Penelope is okay. Let me know if there's anything I can do for either of you."

She displays a sad smile before spinning on her heel and jogging away.

Hayes decides to depart too, detouring by Central Market on the way home. Though he's primarily looking to pick up a few things for his kitchen's inaugural meal, he takes his time to explore the store, blindly following his senses up and down each aisle.

Instrumental music plays overhead, and various aromas waft through the air. Customers push carts brimming full of fresh vegetables, exotic fruits, flavorful coffees, and unique cuts of meat around the store, stopping for the occasional taste test.

A foodie demoing authentic Italian pasta gives him just the inspiration he needs. His menu confirmed, Hayes does another lap around the store to gather the necessary ingredients for chicken parmesan and a few other household staples before calling it a day.

On his way to the checkout, a seasonal display of flowers catches his attention. He selects the perfect bouquet for the perfect woman on his mind.

He scribbles a note on the brown paper wrapping and drops them off on Margaret's doorstep, hoping they will at least bring a smile to her beautiful face.

Hope Penelope gets better soon. Let me know if you need anything. —H

PS: I'm sorry for everything.

At home, Hayes procrastinates on homeowner chores like unpacking boxes and making tough furniture decisions. While he has never been one to *really* care about decor, the fact that his voice echoes in every room proves he needs something to fill the space and make it homier.

Saving those responsibilities for later, he instead focuses on things he *wants* to do, such as rolling dough and simmering vegetables on his new, high-tech stovetop.

His hands sticky and covered in flour, Hayes maneuvers around the spacious kitchen like a doctor who just scrubbed in, avoiding all clean surfaces and extraneous tools. Committed to only de-doughing his hands once, he ignores all incoming notifications, content with addressing them later.

With the messiest part of the process complete and his hands clean, Hayes retrieves his phone and wipes the small beads of sweat growing on his forehead.

> UNKNOWN NUMBER
> *Thank you. You're too kind.*

Despite the unknown number, context clues quickly reveal the sender's identity.

Margaret.

She attaches a photo of the flowers he'd dropped by earlier. Despite wilting a little from sitting outside longer than they should have, they still look beautiful. She arranged them in a fancy vase, something he wouldn't have thought to do, and placed them on her dining table.

Stirring his sauce and preparing to cook the noodles, Hayes fires back.

> HAYES
> *I'm glad you like them. They reminded me of you. How is PG? Can I do anything to help?*

> MARGARET
> *We just got back from the vet. Talk about chaos. She's pretty out of it right now, but she should be fine. Just scary. Thanks for checking in.*

Hayes ponders what it would be like if she were here cooking with him, pretending to be his sous-chef and measuring each ingredient with precision. He pictures them play fighting with flour and dancing around the kitchen to songs of her choosing. He contemplates what she might be wearing right now and what her dinner plans consist of.

> HAYES
> *Good deal, that's good to hear. I was worried about you both. Have you had dinner?*

His stomach growls as he reads the message and shifts around various pots and pans. As he presses send, a rush of adrenaline races through him.

Before he even has a chance to set his phone down, Margaret responds.

> MARGARET
> *No*
>
> HAYES
> *Would you like to come over?*

He sends the message while mindlessly stirring his scratch-made marinara without even considering how inconsiderate the proposition makes him seem. Hitting the counter in frustration, he formulates a quick follow-up to recover.

> HAYES
> *Or can I bring you something? I know you probably don't want to leave Penelope...*

Fortunately for Hayes, Margaret accepts his offer. The timing is perfect, as the pasta is al dente, and the chicken has just reached its ideal state in the oven. Hayes takes his time packaging up the food to ensure it stays intact and warm on the drive over. He scans the selection of wines he purchased earlier in the day and slipped a couple of bottles of red into the bag—a perfect pairing.

> HAYES
> *On my way... be there in fifteen ish.*

On the drive over, Hayes thinks through all his talking points, outlining the information as if he's rehearsing for a commencement speech. With a laundry list worth of apologies to make and questions to answer, Hayes wishes he hadn't been such a coward and approached this conversation months ago.

Margaret is peeking out from behind the door as he approaches. Hayes is certain if he were to look up "all-natural beauty," her picture would be the top hit.

"Hi again," he says, his eyes locked on hers and his hands full.

"Two deliveries in one day? I must be special," she teases, relieving him of one of the dishes. Bringing the foil-covered casserole dish to her face, Margaret inhales deeply and moans. "Oh my gosh! This smells amazing!" She heads for the kitchen, continuing to appreciate the aroma billowing from his masterpiece.

Making his way through the apartment, Hayes evaluates it differently than before. Rather than observing her pictures or knick-knacks, he focuses on how it makes him feel. Cozy. Welcome. Happy. The opposite of his new abode, which is stiff and sterile. Recognizing the importance of the little details, he makes a mental note to add a few pillows to his Wayfair order and press *submit* when he gets home.

"I hope it tastes as good as it smells! I haven't cooked much lately, so I felt a little rusty." Hayes sets the dishes down, trying to break the ice and manage her expectations.

His stomach was growling audibly, and Hayes motioned toward the food. As he lifts up the corner to sneak a peek, he asks, "Are you hungry? I can fix our plates," wanting to take as much stress off her as possible.

"Yes. Starving." She reaches down to pick up Penelope Grace and cradles her like a baby.

The little pup has two shaved legs and gauze covering her entire torso. "Tough little girl, you've got there," he says, gesturing to the dog as he opens each cabinet in search of plates. He gets lucky on his third try, retrieving two from the cupboard.

"She's a trooper, that's for sure," Margaret says, giving Penelope a gentle kiss. "Apparently, someone left the gate open between the big and little dog play areas. She tried to sneak an extra treat, and one of the big dogs just wasn't having it. Pounced on her and wouldn't let go."

He listens to her shaky voice tell the story, imagining how scary it must have been for both Penelope and Margaret. "That's horrible! I'm so glad she's okay!"

"Me too," Margaret agrees, setting the dog down in favor of her loaded plate.

She leads the way to the small patio adjacent to the living room, and Hayes follows. Twinkly lights illuminate the space, and the small two-top table is preset with silverware and water glasses.

"'Wow," Hayes says in awe, "This is fancy!"

"Well, I needed something to distract me from obsessing over Penelope, and this seemed like the best use of my time," Margaret justifies.

Penelope Grace finds her spot under the table between their feet. Moving around sluggishly after her long day, she's much more subdued than in their previous encounters.

Before finding his own seat, Hayes says, "I brought wine too… Would you like some?"

Her eyes light up as if he's told her she just won the lottery. "You really did think of everything, didn't you?"

He scurries back inside for the bottle, an opener, and some glasses from her sophisticated bar cart display in the dining area. Swiftly, he opens the bottle and pours them each a glass.

"Thank you," Margaret says with soft eyes and a neutral expression.

"Anything for you."

Hayes watches her cheeks take on a different shade of pink as she swallows her first sip of the red blend.

Focused on his plate, Hayes digs in. He allows a few beats to pass before returning his utensils to their original home, his appetite no longer present.

"Listen, Margaret," he says, shifting in his chair to meet her gaze directly. "Words cannot even begin to express how truly and deeply sorry I am for everything."

She takes another bite of pasta but doesn't even pretend to hide her big brown eyes, tears threatening to spill over.

"I want you to know I never intended to hurt you." Hayes fiddles with the stem of his wine glass as a distraction. "Honestly, I felt like you deserved more, better than the version of me I could offer at the time," he shares, his voice seeping with honesty. "And, to some extent, I still do."

Fearful of digging a deeper hole for himself, Hayes stuffs his face with food to avoid rambling. Time stands still as he waits for Margaret to respond; the clinking of forks against plates and the occasional car driving by are the only things filling the silence.

She swirls her wine around for aeration and folds her hands on the table. "Look, I'm willing to hear you out, but I'm not making any promises either."

Hayes senses strength and conviction in her voice. Different than before. And while he finds her newfound confidence attractive, it makes him nervous. Antsy.

His palms sweating and right knee bouncing up and down, Hayes grapples with what to say next.

"That's fair. I can't expect you to." Staring into the lights, he takes a sip from his glass.

Then, just as he rehearsed on the way over, Hayes tells her everything, sparing no details. While she nods along and inserts the occasional affirmative hum, the conversation is heavily one-sided.

Hayes tells her everything from how he landed his job to how he first learned of his mother's stage-four breast cancer diagnosis a few years ago. He expresses how the pandemic brought him closer to home and how her declining health kept him there. He explained their routine after he started traveling for work again, flying in late every Thursday evening and out after lunch on Sunday.

He explains how, fortunately, his mom responded well to her treatments and remained in good spirits far longer than the doctors estimated. "Everything was great... until my brother called me out of the blue one day a few months back and said something was wrong with *my dad*. That's when everything went downhill."

Pausing, he collects himself and makes eye contact with Margaret for the first time since starting his monologue. Observing the low level of both their glasses, he retrieves the bottle to top them off as a little intermission.

Hayes then proceeds to describe the circumstances surrounding his father's emergency and sudden passing, as well as the toll it took on him, his brothers, and most significantly, his mom. "She had been so strong, and in hindsight, I realize she was being strong for him. Once he passed, she felt like she had no reason to fight." He pauses. Then, with his volume and intensity dialed back considerably, he says, "We had less than a week with her after that."

At the sound of Margaret's sniffles, he looks at her again and wipes a tear from her cheek. A lump forming in his own throat, he swallows deeply and condenses the last part of the story.

"And after that, I was just in a deep, dark hole. I didn't even feel like myself. I was still living in my parents' home, my childhood bedroom, but it felt foreign. And I know it sounds crazy and totally ridiculous, but I lost my phone in the airport trying to get to Chicago. I hadn't backed up, so I lost most of my contacts." He rolls his eyes, acknowledging the insanity of it all.

She cracks a smile but still doesn't say anything.

"It's a shitty excuse, I know. I wanted to reach out the whole time because I missed you, Margaret," he says, reaching for her hand across the small bistro table. "But truthfully, I could not fathom worrying about anyone besides myself. It's selfish, but it's true." He gives her fingers a gentle squeeze. "The thought of losing someone else close to me, the thought of losing you, just made me sick. I couldn't do it."

He leans forward in his chair, closer to her now than he's been the whole time. "I didn't feel like myself, and I sure as hell didn't feel like I deserved you. I could hardly look in the mirror, knowing the pain I had caused you by just running off like that."

He studies her, holding both of her hands in his, and wraps up his confession. "But now, I'm here. With you. And it's the only place I want to be."

CHAPTER 23

The effects of the wine combined with the emotional story Hayes just delivered have Margaret spinning. She can only make sense of all she has just learned in one-word increments.

Wow.
Dad.
Mom.
Pain.
Heartache.
Embarrassment.
Chicago.
Phone.
Selfish.
Chaos.
Love.
Him.
Here.
Wow.

Time seemingly stood still. Margaret dabs the salty tears from her cheeks and runs her fingers through her stringy hair, ashamed of every negative thought she had about the man sitting across from her.

Speechless, she reflects on how things aren't always as they seem and wishes she hadn't been so quick to jump to conclusions. You never *truly* know all that's going on behind the scenes. Sometimes there *is* an explanation, and not everything is an *excuse*.

"I... I'm so sorry, Hayes," Margaret finally manages, shaking her head in disbelief and struggling to articulate her empathy. "You are so strong, and I have no doubt both of your parents are beyond proud of the man they raised."

"Thank you. I hope so," he says, nodding solemnly. "I think they also would have wanted me to be honest with you, though. From the get-go." He drums his fingers along the tabletop and, looking off into the distance, adds, "My mom would wring my neck if she knew all I put you through."

A half smile appears on his face just before he adds, "Plus, no secrets would've made things a helluva lot easier..."

Dad. Mom.

Hugging her knees into her chest, she dismisses his sly attempt at humor. "I j-just can't believe all you went through." She reflects on the strength and courage he displayed while she was wallowing in self-pity for hardly any good reason at all.

Suppressing her regret, she continues. "I wish I'd been there for you... Your world was literally falling apart, and I..." Margaret trails off, unable to even finish the comparison. She rests her head on her fist, avoiding eye contact.

Heartache. Embarrassment.

"I feel horrible for jumping to such selfish conclusions." She lets out a bitter and embarrassing laugh. While Margaret doesn't elaborate any further, she continues to beat herself up internally, regretting her selfishness and feeling guilty for ever thinking so poorly of him.

"You had every right to, though," Hayes interjects. "I didn't make this easy on you, and I don't want you to think your pain is invalid just because of these really shitty circumstances."

Another tear escapes her right eye and trails down the forearm currently serving as her head's kickstand.

Phone. Selfish. Chaos.

"In a way, I was selfish too," Hayes admits. "I took the easy way out all along, only thinking about what would be best for me. Not you," he says, drawing in even closer. "And not us either."

Us.

"I shouldn't have kept secrets. I should have come clean." He shakes his head, his expression full of regret. "And I should've backed up my damn phone."

This time, his humor makes her giggle, allowing a fraction of the pent-up tension in her muscles to release.

"That would've been nice," Margaret agrees, giving him a playful shove.

Love. Him. Here.

The dark sky and string lights make his eyes shimmer, various shades of blue like the ocean. He explores her features, from her hair to her eyes to her lips and everywhere in between. It takes a second for Margaret to realize her eyes are following a similar pattern, seeping with wonder and desire.

The gap between them slowly disintegrates, and anticipation takes its place. A gust of wind blows through, giving Margaret a good whiff of his cologne. She could recognize that scent anywhere.

His eyes are now downcast, zeroed in on her lips like a sniper on his target. Her heart is beating rapidly, meaning it's only a matter of time until her body is drawn to his like a magnet.

Margaret's eyelids fall shut at the exact moment their lips make contact.

The kiss begins slow, soft, and gentle, the occasional saltiness of a lingering tear finding its way into the mix.

Sniffling, Margaret pulls away, her eyes still locked on his. Remaining as close as they can be without touching, Margaret savors the feeling of his breath against her skin. He gently traces her face with the back of his hand as the still of the night amplifies the sounds of critters in the background.

Margaret continues to study his expression—twisted with pain, sadness, hope, and love. Though nonverbally, they exchange understanding and forgiveness, and their lips collide again.

Attempting to make up for lost time and all the nights she spent dreaming of this particular moment, Margaret finds herself almost breathless. Leaning back in her chair, she smiles, savoring the tingling feeling and sweet taste of him on her lips.

Hayes glances between the two wine glasses, sitting idle on the table. Both are empty again, a faint red tint lingering around the edges. He shifts his gaze back to her and says, "I brought another bottle… would you like me to open it?"

Her lips are turned up at the edges, and her fingers dance against the arm of the chair in excitement. "Always so prepared," she responds.

Hayes is inside before she even finishes her statement, as if he already knows the answer. Moments later, he reappears and presents the bottle for her approval like a waiter at a five-star restaurant. "Madame," he teases. "Do you approve?"

"Indeed," Margaret says firmly, playing along with his charade.

He opens their second bottle as if he *once was* a waiter in a five-star restaurant and pours her a little taste to ensure it meets her standards. Margaret pretends to study the glass and its contents, swirling it around, observing the color in the light, and inhaling deeply before finally taking a sip. Her expression is serious as she searches for the proper review.

"It's excellent, sir. Thank you." Sitting her glass down, she retrieves his. "Would you have a drink with me?" she asks, continuing the act.

"It would be my pleasure," he says with a wink like that had been his plan all along.

Hayes pours his glass and hoists it in the air as he resumes his seat.

"To us," he says.

Clinking her glass to his, she echoes the sentiment, hardly believing the words with her own ears. "To us."

The hours fly as Margaret and Hayes continue to catch up on the other's life. While on the one hand, it seems preposterous to have reconciled so quickly, on the other hand, she can't imagine anything different.

It was always meant to be this way.

Margaret is startled and brought back to reality by Penelope Grace's pained whine from beneath them. Having lost track of time, Margaret realizes she's overdue for her next dose of pain meds.

Margaret stands unsteadily. "I need to get her some medicine and take her out really quickly. I'll be right back."

Escorting the fragile, recovering pup outside, Margaret wrangles with the many thoughts running through her mind. Despite doing her best to ignore the world around her, she can't help but hear the giggles escaping from a gaggle of girls a few buildings down or the car door slamming behind her. She dismisses both, following close behind Penelope Grace until a shadow catches her eye.

Spinning around, ever cautious of her surroundings, Margaret is surprised to see her favorite neighbor.

"Hello, lady! Didn't expect to see you out tonight!" Britt says.

"Likewise! What are you doing out at this time of night? Shouldn't you be at work or sleeping?" Margaret asks.

"Well," Britt says, drawing out the word and calling attention to the miniskirt she's sporting. "I just went on a date!" she squeals, bobbing up and down like a whack-a-mole.

Far from her typical navy scrubs.

Margaret's ears perk up, eager to know *all* the details. "OMG," she says, pulling Penelope Grace closer. "Tell me more."

Standing outside Margaret's apartment, Britt supplies her a brief rundown of who, what, when, where, and how. Margaret interjects the occasional clarifying question, beaming with excitement.

"Anyway, he was great. I have a good feeling about him," Britt concludes, glancing through the window into Margaret's kitchen. Her head cocks to the side slightly, causing Margaret to track her gaze. Both are surprised to see Mr. Americano leaning over the sink, his sleeves rolled up and dishes in hand.

"What the hell! Enough about me! What is going on here?" Britt asks, gesturing toward Margaret's dinner guest with suspicious eyes and a sneaky smile.

Thankful for the night sky hiding her pink cheeks, Margaret says, "I'll fill you in tomorrow. You are not going to believe it."

Britt fake pouts but agrees to check-in later. She gives PG a few sympathy pets and then heads inside.

By the time Margaret and Penelope return to the kitchen, Hayes's fingers have wrinkled, and all the dishes have been put away. He is standing in the kitchen, propped against the counter. Margaret wraps her arms tightly around his waist from behind, pressing her chest against his toned back.

While earlier, they had been confined by the arms of their chairs and the nearby table, there are no barriers between them now.

Other than their clothes.

* * *

Margaret wakes up to Hayes standing next to her bed with two iced americanos and a pair of scones in hand. He studies each cup, deciphering which one is for her and which for him.

Giggling and reaching for one of the two drinks, she says, "Aren't they the same? I'm not picky!" Hayes deliberately hands her the *other* cup, turning it around to reveal a message scribbled on the side.

> I HAVE WAITED FOR THIS MOMENT SINCE YOU MET;)
> COME SEE ME! XOXO
> ++ ADDED SOMETHING EXTRA THIS AM. ENJOY!

While the note isn't signed, it is unmistakably from Lucy.

Margaret's heart swells at the thought of her quirky friend. "Man, I've missed her!" She shakes her head and laughs.

She stabs the straw onto the bed, attempting to break through the paper wrapping. "Thanks for the treat! This is by far the best way to start my day."

"Anything for you," Hayes says, sitting down on the edge next to her.

Despite having spent a few nights together, this is the only morning they've ever shared. While it could easily feel forced or awkward, Margaret is struck with how surprisingly normal and natural it is. Like home.

He makes this place feel like home.

The realization takes her back to her first-ever journal entry.

"What time is it anyway?" Margaret asks, still drowsy and out of touch. "I guess I should let Penelope out," she says, peeling herself out of bed and looking around the room for her Uggs.

Hayes stops her by placing a gentle hand on her knee. "It's okay. I already took care of her. She enjoyed going on a field trip too!"

Happy to curl back up under the covers, Margaret says, "Thank you, you're too kind."

"And," Hayes says, dragging out the word with a mischievous grin on his face, "I might have gotten her a little treat…"

Margaret bites her straw and waits for his confession.

"She requested a pup cup, and, quite frankly, I couldn't resist. Gotta stay on her good side!"

Smart man.

Reaching for her cup, Hayes asks for a sip of her *special* drink, practically laying on top of her in the process. "I wanna know what all of this vanilla nonsense is about."

His eyes light up as the liquid gold makes contact with his tastebuds. "Dang! Why doesn't Lucy hook *me* up with that?"

"Maybe you'll get lucky next time," Margaret teases, putting the cup on her nightstand and rolling over to position *herself* on top of *him*.

CHAPTER 24

After Hayes leaves to tend to things at home, Margaret tidies up her own space and prepares to break the news to her fan club. Mr. Americano is back and better than ever.

She starts with Britt, generally her most supportive and pro-Mr. Americano friend. Margaret opts to give her spiel a trial run with the easiest to please, hoping some practice will allow her to get it under control before she tries to sell the others on her man.

> MARGARET
> *Hey, girl. Wanna go get a mani?*
>
> BRITT
> *You know I'm in. Meet outside in five?*

Giving the message a quick thumbs up, Margaret throws on a casual athleisure outfit and makes her bed, still in total disarray from last night's—and this morning's—mayhem.

Their favorite nail salon, known for serving bottomless complimentary cocktails, is located on the north side of town, fifteen minutes from where they usually hang out. On the car ride over, Britt elaborates on her Bumble date and the events that have transpired since their conversation last night.

"We have literally been texting nonstop," she says, glancing in all her mirrors and merging onto the highway. "He already asked me out again! I can't believe it!"

Her genuine enthusiasm reminds Margaret of how she felt about Hayes on day one. *Serious. Different.*

"I love it, I love it, I love it," Margaret affirms. "What are y'all doing next?"

Snickering, Britt says, "He asked me to go to Fiesta Texas, and I am low-key so excited about it. I haven't been since we went in high school for a physics field trip!"

"That is so fun and adventurous. A guy's date ideas say a lot about him, so this is a good sign," Margaret affirms.

The girls pick out their colors, pale pink for Britt and lavender for Margaret, navigate to their assigned seats, and order their first mimosas. Before Margaret can even roll up her sleeves to soak off her last set, Britt is already asking her question after question.

"How did you start talking again? Were you even going to say anything if I hadn't seen him in your kitchen? He better have had a good excuse. OMG, did he stay the night?" As the questioning escalates, her pace quickens, and she hardly takes a breath.

Inserting the occasional groan as the nail tech prods at her cuticles, Margaret rehashes yesterday's events beginning with their coffee shop run-in, including Penelope's emergency, Hayes's confession, and the aftermath. While her story teeters on the edge of sounding like a sales pitch, Britt's investment and emotional reaction indicate it's effective, nonetheless.

"That is insane," Britt says, practically speechless. "I wanted to believe he had a good excuse and wasn't willfully ghosting you, but guys can be such assholes these days, so you never know." She shakes her head as if she's experienced it herself a time or two. "You just never know."

"Me too. I felt so small the whole time he was explaining everything because I was so embarrassed for jumping to such a selfish conclusion. Never in my life have I experienced such a things-aren't-as-they-always-seem situation," Margaret says, wincing in pain as the acetone seeps into fresh cuts courtesy of her manicurist.

Toasting her plastic dixie cup with Margaret's, Britt says, "Amen, sista," and slurps up the refreshing citrus. "I'm glad he came back around. You know…"

Margaret throws a puzzled look. "What?"

"Maybe," Britt pauses again, her tone serious and calculated, "we can go on a double date!"

Margaret lets out a big sigh of relief. "You had me panicked! I can't handle any more dramatic conversations for at least six months. But yes, I hear you. We can make that happen pronto."

* * *

When Amanda rolls into work a little after 8:30 on Monday morning, Margaret is already positioned at her desk, firing away email after email.

"Well, well, well," she says, approaching Margaret's self-assigned cubicle. "Look at you all fancy and chipper this morning. What's going on?" She perches on the edge of Margaret's desk, peering down at her ever so slightly. "I haven't seen you this upbeat since..." Amanda trails off. "Since I don't know when."

Margaret's hair, for once, is freshly curled, her makeup complete, and her blouse appropriately steamed. Closing her laptop and spinning her conventional office chair in Amanda's direction, Margaret says, "Well, do I have an update for you."

She launches into her speech, more polished than her first run-through yesterday with Britt. She hits all the high points, in chronological order this time, and adds in the occasional supporting detail when Amanda's expression leans skeptical.

Before Margaret even finishes, she notices Amanda's perfectly lined and shadowed eyes are glossy. "Are you okay? Did I say something?"

Shaking her head and dabbing the damp area around her eyes, Amanda says, "No, not at all. I-I just truly can't imagine what he was going through." She sniffles. "I thought my world was ending when my parents were in a car wreck together a few years ago, and they both survived! I can't imagine his pain in losing both of them so unexpectedly and so traumatically."

Her sympathy sends an ache to Margaret's heart. Her own parents are top of mind again. Margaret pledges to herself she will give them a call later, acutely aware of how blessed she is to still have them.

"I know. Truly unimaginable."

Margaret continues with her update in a more positive and hopeful tone than she's had in weeks.

"I love seeing you so happy." Amanda smiles sweetly and studies Margaret's face. "I hope I never see you take a faux walk of shame again," she teases.

Before they switch gears to talk about more professional topics, Amanda throws one more question in the mix. "Well, I can't ship this unless I've met him, so you better get on it, sister!"

Noted.

* * *

Two out of three updates were delivered. Margaret is relieved but knows the next one will be a doozy. She treats herself to a long overdue trip to The Brew on her way home from work to mentally prepare.

An overzealous Lucy demanding to know every detail greets her as soon as the door swings open.

Make that two of four updates delivered.

Lucy, enthusiastic as ever, has changed her hair color and added a piercing or two since Margaret last saw her. Behind the counter, she instinctively whips up a special iced americano for Margaret and a dirty chai tea latte for herself without instruction.

Whizzing around through the swinging door that separates the baristas from the patrons, Lucy hastily sets the cups down and throws her arms around Margaret. "I've been waiting for you to get back in here!" she says, stepping back and studying Margaret's features like a sculptor admiring their creation.

"I know, I know. Trust me, I've wanted to, but there's just been so much going on…"

"Yeah, yeah, yeah, I know," Lucy says. "Heard all about it yesterday from *him*, but now I need to hear it from *you*!" She plops down on a worn leather loveseat in the middle of The Brew, and Margaret follows suit.

Sinking into the couch, Margaret is struck by how foreign it feels. This seat, front, center, and comfy, couldn't be more opposite from her traditional straight-back wooden chair in the corner. The vibes are much cozier here, a product of both the furniture and her friend.

"I wish you could've seen him in here the other morning. He was so giddy," Lucy says, shrugging and smiling sweetly. "He's been coming here for months, long before you moved here, and I have *never* seen him like that. *Ever*," she emphasizes.

Her words make Margaret feel special and validate this isn't all a figment of her imagination.

"I think I should get credit for this little love story," Lucy says, wiggling her eyebrows. "I know I didn't technically set it up but without me making your strong little drinks..." She pauses to turn her nose up at Margaret's americano and delightfully sip on her latte, "it would never have happened!"

"Fair point. You can add 'matchmaker' to your resume!"

Drawing an imaginary checkmark in the air with her finger, Lucy says, "Success!"

They share a few more laughs and life updates before Lucy says, "Well, as much as it pains me, I ought to get back to it. But don't be a stranger!" Walking away, she throws a peace sign over her shoulder and disappears behind the swinging doors. Moments later, Lucy pops up on the other side with her coffee-stained apron and welcoming smile, ready to resume her barista—and apparently matchmaking—duties.

With her legs folded underneath her on the couch, Margaret pulls up the group chat, preparing herself for what is to come.

He is worth it.

While the wedding drama is still a sensitive topic and source of frustration for Margaret, it's now more so because of *how* her friends handled it than *what* it was really about. With time, she has come to appreciate her friends' concern and recognizes they were *trying* to look out for her.

Since it all went down, though, the quad has had many a conversation about the situation and made a pact to handle things differently going forward.

Wedging out the painful memories in favor of happy news, Margaret sends her first message.

> MARGARET
> *Hey, ladies! Miss y'all <3*
> *I have a little update...*

She snaps a quick photo of her drink, The Brew logo etched into the side and sends it as a clue.

> CAROLINE
> *Do tell...*

> TESS
> *I'm about to head into a meeting, but I want all the tea! Can we Facetime tonight and hear it live?*

> MARGARET
> *Works for me!*

The others emphasize her message in agreement and settle on 8 p.m. While Margaret is eager to tell the story face to face, gauge their reactions in real-time and minimize the risk of a silly text misunderstanding, waiting a few *hours,* rather than just ripping the band-aid off now, makes her anxious.

Relocating again, Margaret distracts herself with unanswered emails and chores around the apartment, looking for anything to keep her from overthinking how this might go.

Since the winter season is giving way to more pleasant spring air, Margaret sets up on her patio again tonight. Her phone strategically propped up against an outdoor citronella candle, Margaret activates the Facetime call with a shaky hand.

She hugs her legs into her chest and rests her chin on her knee for comfort, wrestling with anxiety as she waits for her friends to join. On the one hand, she feels irrational because these are the people she should be *most* comfortable with. But on the other, she is sure she's about to drop a bombshell and considering their prior experiences, it might not go well.

Her thoughts are interrupted by a cheerful Tess hopping on with a wave, followed closely by Susannah, already bedded down for the evening, and Caroline posted up in yet another high-rise hotel on vacation.

Of course. Seems about right.

Talking over each other, they exchange greetings and compliments, all of which go unacknowledged.

Before diving into the deep end, Margaret asks, "Sus! How are you doing? We're getting down to the wire!"

Susannah flips the camera around, revealing her elevated feet and the heating pad beneath her. "I'm counting down, that's for sure. In the home stretch!" she says hopefully.

"I can't wait to meet my little honorary niece!" Tess cheers, rapidly clapping her hands.

"I got her *the* cutest outfit today in New York," Caroline adds. "It's going to be perfect for her first ladies' night."

"I'm almost as excited for you all to meet her as I am!" Susannah says. "But, enough about me and Little Bit. Let's cut to the chase!"

Inhaling deeply, Margaret says, "Well…" She takes an exaggerated pause before letting an uncomfortable laugh escape and admitting, "This is a lot harder than I thought it would be."

She tries to read the girls' faces but struggles to interpret their body language through the phone, thinking, again, how much easier this would all be if they were still roommates.

"It's okay. Take your time," Tess says.

"We're here for you, no matter what it is," Caroline assures her.

Margaret tries again, getting a little further this time, covering their coffee shop run-in and Penelope's scare.

The girls get hung up on Penelope's status, panicking that something is seriously wrong with their fur niece. To ease their concerns, Margaret retrieves PG from her bed as proof she's on the mend.

"Anyway," she says, resuming her story. "After everything went down with Penelope, I left in a hurry. By the time we got home, he had dropped off some flowers for us and a short but sweet note."

She's interrupted by a series of 'aww's' from her audience, but she presses on. She shares how he ended up spending hours, though she doesn't admit all night, at her apartment, and recounts the nuances of their conversation and reunion.

"Essentially, he's been to hell and back in the last few months. His dad suffered a brain aneurysm," the girls gasp, "and ended up passing. On top of that, his mom was battling stage-four breast cancer this whole time—"

She sees their jaws fall further open and their eyes grow larger.

"So, when his dad died, she kinda gave up too. They passed away within a week of one another."

The girls express their heartache for Hayes and his family, sending their condolences and expressing the unfathomableness of the situation.

"Needless to say, he's had a lot going on. All those weekends he was gone, he was taking care of his mom and doing chores around the house for his dad."

Margaret can see the pieces falling into place for them, just as they did for her. "I know. It makes so much sense now. I feel *horrible* for all the things I said and thought about him. It makes me sick."

"It's not your fault, though. Why didn't he just say so? You totally would have supported him!" Tess says, her hesitancy and reluctance to buy this version of events evident.

Margaret explains the reasoning and justification around it all, proud of herself for asking those same questions. The probing and follow-ups continue. But this time, unlike their previous Mr. Americano-related conversations, Margaret *actually* has the answers. By the end, the skepticism has evaporated, and support and joy are in its place.

"So," Caroline says, a sweet smile shaping her picture-perfect dimples. "You know I have to ask…"

Margaret raises her eyebrows, unsure where Caroline is taking them next.

"When can we meet him?"

The others tack on their eagerness, hope oozing through each of their voices.

"Ugh," Tess says. "I wish we could be spontaneous like the good old days."

"Me too," Susannah says, shifting uncomfortably, her face in anguish. "When we could just make plans for the next weekend and have a blast no matter what."

"I mean…" Tess follows up. "I'm free next weekend…"

Caroline's face disappears from the screen as she says, "I think I am too. Double-checking as we speak."

Anticipation bubbling inside her, Margaret volunteers her availability as well.

"I can hardly move," Susannah says. "But as long as I don't have a baby between now and then, I'm free, too!"

"OMG. Are we really doing this?" Caroline asks, her face back on the screen.

Excitement erupts from the girls like lava from a volcano. They talk over one another again, seemingly unfazed by the lack of cohesion or dialogue.

They briefly outline an itinerary, outfit plans, and accommodations. Margaret offers for everyone to stay with her, prefacing it may be a *little cramped* and comparing her apartment to the overcrowded condo they stayed in for spring break a few years back. This anecdote earns her a few good laughs and makes her grin ear to ear, her cheeks pinching in the corners.

"I can't believe this! I am so excited for you all to meet him!"

They say their goodbyes and goodnights, promising to chat again in the next few days. Ending the call, Margaret picks up Penelope Grace and says, "Eeeek! Your aunties are coming to town!"

CHAPTER 25

It only takes a few days for Margaret, Hayes, and Penelope to establish a routine. They spend every evening together, rotating between each of their homes and various local hangouts.

When Margaret isn't snuggled up next to or enjoying a meal with Hayes, she spends her time prepping for her upcoming guests. She happily takes care of all her adult duties by dusting, vacuuming, sweeping, and laundering so that by Friday, only a few chores remain.

"You'll pick up the dry cleaning on your way home, right?" Hayes asks.

"Yep!" Margaret says, rising to her tiptoes to kiss him goodbye.

"See you later!" Hayes calls over his shoulder, closing the door and locking it with his own key.

She watches him leave her apartment, dressed as sharp as usual and like he's done it a million times before. Though it's only been a few days, their worlds and habits are already intertwined in the best way possible.

Margaret sips on yet another surprise iced americano courtesy of Hayes and smiles. His justification for specialty coffee this morning being, "It's Friday."

I could get used to this.

Knowing her guests are scheduled to arrive soon after she gets off work, Margaret spends extra time in front of the mirror this morning, precisely perfecting her look. Even with her prolonged beauty session, she still manages to make it to the office ahead of schedule.

Look at that punctuality!

When Amanda finally strolls in, looking a little worse for wear, she admits to having a wild Thursday night. This, however, does not deter her from agreeing to tonight's festivities anyway.

"I just had one too many at Lush-ous last night, no big deal," she whispers so only Margaret can hear. "But don't you worry, I wouldn't miss the big night for anything!"

Since Margaret broke the news to everyone about rekindling her relationship with Hayes, the hype has been building. Amanda initially coined the phrase "big night," but Margaret has since shared it with all other invested parties. Considering all of Margaret's worlds are colliding, she must admit it does make for a rather fitting title.

Huddled up at Margaret's desk, "collaborating," Amanda asks what she plans to wear this evening.

"I have no idea," Margaret says, mentally rifling through everything in her closet. Already anticipating her frustration and the "nothing looks good on me" debate, she says, "I need to figure that out…"

"What's the vibe?" Amanda inquires, her hand resting on her chin.

"I assume we'll go to Fred's, at least first, mainly because it's so easy and great for big groups. After that, I have no idea, though."

"Oh. So, there's gonna be an *after*?" Amanda shifts in her seat with her arms crossed and one eyebrow raised.

"Cannot confirm nor deny," Margaret says, her head bowed, fingers on the keyboard, and focus on her computer.

Based on her ferocious typing and serious expression, one would assume she's doing just that, but her search history says otherwise:

San Antonio weather tonight
Cute February going-out outfits
Best outdoor bars in San Antonio
Date night outfit inspo

When Lacey gives everyone the green light to head out early, Margaret cleans up her desk area in record time. On the way home, she swings by the liquor store, floral shop, and dry cleaners—a combination of stops that solidifies she's officially reached adulthood.

To her surprise, Hayes is already at the apartment when she arrives, in the kitchen whipping up an assortment of hors d'oeuvres for their guests. Meanwhile, Penelope sits politely behind him, her paws crossed for a treat or two.

"Hey, you," he says, chopping up various vegetables with smooth precision.

"Hi! It smells amazing in here!" Margaret says, kissing his cheek and searching around for the source of the aroma. "How was your day?"

"Good, but better now," Hayes responds sincerely. He places the knife down, wipes his hands on a nearby kitchen towel, and embraces her in a hug.

Her head nuzzled into his neck, Margaret inhales and tightens her grip just slightly. "Mine too," she agrees before pulling away. "What is that smell? I want to eat it right now!"

"Brie. It's baking as we speak."

He's so nonchalant.

Sneaking a peek through the oven door, she says, "You are amazing. I can't wait to try it!"

She places the recently purchased bottles of wine in the fridge and retreats to her room to freshen up. Just as she's put on her fifth outfit of the try-on session, Tess's voice echoes through the apartment.

"Knock, knock! The party has arrived!" Having let herself in, she enters with Ben close behind, his arms full of bags, baked goods, and more alcohol.

Running to the door, Margaret exclaims, "I'm so glad you're here!" She engulfs Tess in an embrace first before acknowledging her husband. "And hi, Ben! Thanks for being the pack mule again," Margaret adds, reaching in for their trademark side hug. "Make yourself at home."

A millisecond later, still standing in the hallway, Tess is already poking her in the side, wiggling her eyebrows and whispering, "Are you gonna introduce me or not?"

With rosy cheeks, Margaret guides their first two guests through the narrow hallway into the kitchen. Hayes, cleaning off the countertop, tosses the towel off to the side and extends his hand to Ben.

"Well, I guess we need formal introductions!" Margaret says. She gestures between three of her favorite people to reinforce the connection, but they've already hit it off.

Success.

She repeats this same exercise again when Caroline and Logan arrive, followed by Susannah and Stephen. By round three, she's feeling slight déjà vu. But then again, it could be the second glass of wine Hayes poured her that she has consumed on an empty stomach. Perhaps time will tell.

Each of the girls takes a casual turn speaking one-on-one with Hayes. While it could seem forced or contrived, he doesn't seem fazed. Margaret does her best to stay in earshot, available to step in and interject at the drop of a hat, but it isn't needed. Each of them talks to him like he's been a part of the group forever.

I knew they would love him.

Moving the party to Fred's, Margaret and the gang claim an extra-long picnic table on the patio. Amanda was waiting for their arrival so everyone knew everyone after *another* round of introductions.

One big happy family.

Per Britt's request, the group kicks off the evening with a round of pickle shots and a triple order of cheese fries. "Go big or go home," Margaret overheard her say to their waiter.

It doesn't take long for the group to split into boys versus girls. Hayes stands at the other end of the table, telling a story the guys seem to be captivated by.

"Margaret! Margaret?" Caroline asks just as Britt says, "Earth to Margaret!" the combination of voices drawing her out of her daze.

Trying to play it cool, she manages, "Y-yes?"

"Whatcha thinkin' about over there, missy?" Amanda teases.

Continuing to stir the pot, Tess adds, "Looks like someone was daydream—"

"Or thinking about someone on the other end of the table," Susannah interrupts with a playful smile.

With her cheeks on fire, Margaret drops her head and leans back on her stool to escape some of the heat.

"Oh, don't be embarrassed," Susannah offers, coming to her rescue. "Happens to me all the time… I can't stop thinking about Stev—"

Caroline cuts her off. "Oh, honey, we don't need to know what you're thinking about… The baby in your belly tells us enough!" The girls laugh, clinking their mugs—and Susannah's lemonade—in the air.

"On a real note," Tess says, redirecting the conversation once more. "I love seeing you like this. It makes me so happy." The others agree, singing Hayes's praises as both her boyfriend and a chef.

As time passes and drinks are downed, the group rotates and intermingles. Though they're only a few hours in, the weekend is already living up to Margaret's impeccably high expectations.

"Ready for a change of scenery?" Hayes asks, whispering in Margaret's ear from behind. His hand is placed squarely on her back, making it impossible to think about the scenery at all.

"Where do you say we go next?" she asks over her shoulder, enjoying his presence.

Glancing around for inspiration, Hayes suggests the piano bar down the river. Following his lead, the group heads for their next stop in pack formation.

"I am *so* excited about this," Caroline says, hanging on to Logan.

"Has anyone ever seen dueling pianists?" Britt asks the uptick in her voice indicating she knows something the others don't.

Everyone in the group says no except for Hayes. Their knowing eyes and fist bump put an eerie feeling in Margaret's gut. "Uh oh, what are we about to get ourselves into?" she asks.

"Don't worry about it," Hayes says, giving her hand a gentle squeeze. "Just have fun!"

IDs checked, hands stamped, and covers paid, they make their way upstairs. Not surprisingly, the guys head straight for the bar, and the girls find the dance floor.

Segregated again, the girls continue to fawn over Hayes, complimenting his looks, maturity, storytelling, background—*essentially everything*. All the while, Margaret blushes, proud to call him hers and foreign to being the center of attention.

"I told you guys!" she says as if they shouldn't have ever doubted her.

A contagion of eye rolls runs through the group. "Should've seen that one coming," Caroline admits.

"You know we were just trying to look out for you. I am *so* glad you proved us wrong!" Tess adds.

Margaret and her closest friends sway from side to side, jamming to current hits, throwbacks, and everything in between. They rotate who buys drinks, who submits the next song request, and who is responsible for filming so they have something to rewatch in the morning.

Amanda and Britt go on stage for a duet while Caroline and Tess scream the lyrics to every song in each other's faces. Susannah calls it an early night, understandably so, blowing a kiss and giving her blessing on the way out. "He is such a keeper. I totally approve."

Her bladder is about to burst, so Margaret makes a run to the restroom. "Wait up!" Tess calls out, weaving her way through the crowd. When Margaret doesn't stop or turn around, Tess results to tugging on the hem of her dress, a cute and colorful number she happened to come across in the deep, dark pits of her closet.

Margaret whips around prepared to sucker punch whoever is trying to feel her up. Relieved to identify Tess as the culprit, she swats at her hand, saying, "You scared the shit out of me!"

Fortunately, there's no line, and the bathroom attendant kindly offers them every service and treatment they can imagine. The girls linger in front of the mirror, appreciating the cool breeze and personal space that the dance floor lacks.

"I don't remember the last time I saw you this happy," Tess says again, her party face replaced with something more serious. "You're glowing," she adds, reaching out to place her hand on Margaret.

Because it's the truth, and she's so glad her friends can see it too. Her eyes well up. "I love him, Tess."

CHAPTER 26

Looking in the mirror as he shaves, Hayes mentally replays the weekend highlight reel—laughing at the guys' jokes, Amanda and Britt's duet on stage, and Margaret's failed attempt to do a leap in the parking lot on their way home.

Considering his last few months, it's no surprise this weekend was the most fun he has had in a long time. The only weekend that even comes close is Sam's bachelor party, which was nearly five years ago. *What a shame.* He rinses his razor and dabs his fresh face dry.

Throwing on some casual clothes, he heads for the door, leaving his still empty and unfurnished house behind in favor of Margaret's cozy space. With shades on and the windows down, he calls his brother to pass the time.

Wes picks up on the second ring. "Hey, man! How's it going?"

One hand on the wheel, the other dangling out the window, Hayes says, "Oh, you know, it's going. How are the girls? Is it spring break yet?"

Wes drones on and on about his daughters, including their upcoming dance recitals, school projects, and field trips—the whole nine yards. "What about you? How's *your girl*?"

Hayes rolls his eyes and lets out a huff, halfway regretting the inquiry about his nieces. Instead of shutting down and avoiding the subject, though, he follows through with the commitment he made to himself that night at Hannigan's. "Well, funny you should ask," he teases, dangling the truth.

"This ought to be good."

"Honestly? She's great. We spent the weekend hanging out with her friends and coworkers. Went to a few bars, ate good, and laughed a lot. You know how it goes." Hayes pauses, reflecting again on the last forty-eight hours. "I can't remember the last time I had so much fun. It was nice."

"Sounds like a blast. I totally understand. I can't remember the last time I went out like that. Sam's bachelor party in Vegas, I guess."

They share a laugh, tossing memories back and forth before Wes inquires about the house and its status.

"It's super nice. The pictures didn't do it justice. Still empty as hell, though," Hayes says, exiting the highway and closing the distance between him and her.

"I feel like I only have stuff in my closet, bathroom, and kitchen," he says, wishing he would've pressed *submit* on that furniture order already.

Wes chuckles. "Ah, let me guess. You're spending more time with *her* than at your brand-spankin' new place?"

Hayes steals a glance at himself in the rearview mirror, verifying the warmth in his cheeks.

The silence speaks for itself. "I'll take that as a yes then," Wes says, laughing again. "I'm happy for you, bro... Mom and Dad would be too."

"Thank you. I like to think so," Hayes says, imagining what it would have been like if they'd had the chance to meet Margaret. "She's a keeper for sure."

"When do you think we'll get to meet her?" Wes asks, just as Hayes parks in the visitor lot outside Margaret's door.

"Soon, I hope. I'll talk to her and see what we can do."

"Sounds good, buddy. Take care."

Hayes is struck by how much Wes sounds like their father. Clearing his throat, he says, "You too. Give my girls a hug."

When he gets inside, Margaret is sitting on the couch with her lips puckered, ready for her kiss. Despite her lounge attire, she still looks stunning. Her hair has some waves in it, and her eyelashes flutter, making her brown eyes look even bigger than usual.

"Hi," she says, her sweet voice quickly becoming his favorite sound.

Hayes scoops her in his arms and tickles her stomach, perfect laughter filling the room.

"I missed you," he says, despite only being gone for a few hours.

"I missed you more." Margaret reaches up to kiss him again. "What do you wanna do today?"

"Be with you," Hayes says instinctively.

She squirms as her cheeks change colors. Glancing through the open blinds in the kitchen, Margaret suggests coffee and a walk along the river to appreciate the beautiful spring weather.

"Works for me… but one thing…" Hayes pauses, sounding nervous and hesitant.

"Yes?" Margaret asks.

"I cannot handle the mediocre place we went to that time. I *need* Lucy."

"I'm appalled you even thought the alternative was an option."

Minutes later, they walk into The Brew, ecstatic to find Lucy standing behind the bar, keying in their orders before either says a word. "It's about time you two got back here!" she teases, reaching over the ledge to give Margaret a hug. She pretends to sneakily whisper in Margaret's ear but uses her normal volume, "I totally manifested this."

Despite the line forming out the door behind them, Margaret and Hayes linger at the counter to chat with Lucy. Margaret does most of the talking while Hayes listens, appreciating her enthusiasm and how she so effortlessly connects with others.

They take the sighs and eye rolls of other caffeine addicts as their cue to move along. It doesn't take long until their order, two iced americanos and *complimentary* pastries courtesy of Lucy, are placed in the pickup area. Their drinks are labeled accordingly—*Mr. Americano and Miss Americano.*

Reading their labels, Margaret rolls her eyes and shakes her head. "Oh, Lucy."

Sitting under a shade tree on their favorite little bench, Hayes extends his arm around Margaret and observes life around them. Coffee drinkers sipping away, spring flowers in full bloom, and the woman he loves sitting next to him.

Turning his attention to Margaret, he observes how the sun brings out various shades of color in her hair. Hayes sweeps a wild strand behind her ear, a small smile forming on his lips.

He hesitates, despite being more confident in what he's about to say than anything else in his life, and says, "I love you, Margaret."

Her eyes sparkle, and her arms instinctively reach for him. When her head is perfectly nestled against his neck, she whispers back, "I love you too, Mr. Americano."

EPILOGUE

EIGHT MONTHS LATER...

The moving team arrives at 8 a.m. on the dot, prepared to load all of Margaret's prepacked, individually labeled boxes. As of today, she will *officially* be roommates with Hayes.

It's been a long time coming considering he asked her to move in on the same day he told her he loved her. While she didn't say no, logistically, she couldn't say yes at the time either. For the last eight months, they have drifted back and forth between one another's places, choosing their accommodations based on convenience.

Penelope Grace is partial to the house, though, because she's given the freedom to run free. She now dreads any time they spend at the apartment, where she's inevitably confined to her leash.

Last week, Hayes brought home a little brother for Penelope Grace as a "welcome home gift"—a fluffy chocolate lab with more energy and sharper teeth than Margaret was prepared for. While Penelope isn't interested at first, they've become fast friends, and Margaret can already tell they will be thick as thieves.

Though the last thing Margaret *wants* to do is unpack all the boxes she just packed less than seventy-two hours ago, she has an incentive. This weekend, the happy couple is hosting a housewarming party and welcoming their friends and family from far and wide to San Antonio. It has been months since they've all been together, so when Hayes suggested they use the new house as an excuse, Margaret quickly obliged.

Fiercely unpacking and breaking down box after box, time flies by, and it is Saturday before she even knows it. And, as it turns out, the "housewarming party" was all a ruse. Everyone but Margaret was in on Hayes's meticulous plan to pop the question.

In the middle of a toast welcoming their guests, Hayes hands off his champagne flute and gets down on one knee. Looking up at Margaret with hopeful and loving eyes, he says, "Margaret, since the moment you tried to steal my coffee, I knew you were special." Giggles escape from the crowd surrounding them, and Margaret's cheeks take on a warmer shade of pink. "The way you love, encourage, support, and challenge me is unlike anything I've ever experienced. You make me a better man and are the highlight of every single one of my days."

He gives her hands a gentle squeeze before continuing. "I want to love you forever, Margaret Parton. Will you marry me?"

Between tears, Margaret manages to chant, "Yes!" triggering cheers from all directions.

Unbeknownst to Margaret, Hayes has been hiding a jaw-dropping emerald-cut diamond on a gold band in his nightstand for over six months. As he slides the finest piece of jewelry she's ever seen on her finger, Margaret is speechless.

In awe and in love.

The next morning, she wakes to Hayes sitting next to her with an iced americano in hand like he has so many times before. This time, Lucy's note on the side reads, *Mrs. Americano.*

Sipping on her delicious coffee, Margaret jots down her journal entry for the previous day while the emotions are still fresh.

The most incredible man I've ever known asked me to marry him! We celebrated with our people, and it was perfect. I can't wait to spend the rest of my days loving him. Everything happens for a reason, and the best is yet to come. XOXO

ACKNOWLEDGMENTS

Before diving headfirst into this journey, I had never really given much thought to the support system writers must have. But now? I understand all too well.

I could not have achieved this dream and crossed "become an author" off my bucket list without my tremendous, multi-faceted support system.

This book is the product of lots of labor and love from not only myself but so many others as well. Thank you for being a part of my team and making *Mr. Americano* possible.

I have to start by thanking Shane for supporting me and my book journey from day one. Ever since my initial Creator Institute call, Shane has believed in me and has been my biggest fan. From reading various drafts to giving me advice on my cover and listening to my rants, he's been there for it all and seen the good, the bad, and the ugly along the way. Thank you for being my real-life romance novel. I couldn't have done this without you.

Thank you to my mom and dad for always encouraging me to shoot for the stars and dream big. Because of you, I know that I can do anything I set my mind to, which apparently means writing a book! Woohoo! Mom, thank you for being my first beta reader, in-house copyeditor, "publicist," and more. Dad, thank you for answering all of my medical questions and being the reason I even know what an americano is… I think it is safe to say Mr. Americano wouldn't exist without you either.

I would be remiss not to acknowledge the star of this whole show, Penelope Grace. She was truly by my side for every single late morning and early night I dedicated to this project. She's seen my work on this book firsthand more than anyone else. She's kept me company, helped me overcome the loneliness and comforted me on more days than I can count. Love you, my little coauthor.

A special shout out to my besties—thank you for being the greatest friends a girl could ask for. From filling out my early questionnaires, being the first to respond to my Facebook posts, and offering beta reader feedback, you all have played a critical role in this process. Thank you for teaching me what it means to be a true friend. You all make me better and inspire me daily.

To the Creator Institute and New Degree Press teams, thank you. This book wouldn't be what it is without your influence and expertise. Special thank you to Eric, Ilia, Michelle, and Megan for pouring into me. Thanks to your editorial help, encouragement, and technical insights, I was able to transform an idea I was excited about into a novel that I'm proud of. To my fellow authors, I'm so glad we were able to share this journey! Knowing that I wasn't on this path alone brought me great peace. I am grateful to be a part of this community.

The ever-talented Maria made designing the cover one of my favorite parts of this entire process. She brought my vision to life more perfectly than I ever dreamed possible. I can't wait to stare at my bookshelf forever.

Special thank you to The Brew Crew—the people that truly made all of this possible—Lauren Abiog, Julia Abrams, Carolyn Anderson, Rene Berkley, Patsy and Glendon Berry, Ruth Bristow, Christina Brown, Sarah Brown, Jennifer Burke, Lisa Byington, Alison Campbell, Cathryn Campbell, Christy Carnes, Caroline and Josh Cole, Jamie Conley, Emily Cooper, Charlotte Corley, Terra Cundieff, Lara Cupit, Tommye Lou Davis, Margaret Dodson, Courtney Fernandez, Jessie Feuerbacher, Suzanne Feuerbacher, Mykayla Fontaine, Shannon Gallagher, Bonnie and John Garcia, Jami Gladden, Shannon Guttry, Reece Hageman, Madison Hankins, Kim Hardy, Kathy Hayes, Lynne and Kirk Henderson, Sarah Henderson, Margaret Hill, Bettie Holcomb, Cortney Holcomb, Dustin Holcomb, Kim and Matt Holcomb, Rosemary Holcomb, Susan Holcomb, Ginger Holley, Justine Hopkins, Shane Hopkins, Phyllis Jolley Smith, Pat Keel, Sydney King, Joe Knox, Eric Koester, Jill Laing, Danna Lindley, Jamie Lindsey, Gary and Leighann Lindsey, Linda and Russell Lindsey, Sarah Lindsey, Amy Littlejohn, Sydney Long, Marsha Mills, April Mitchell, Molly Thompson, Annika Neldeberg, Jan Ortman, Lauren Osborne, Laurie Perkins, Shannon Perkins, Kevin Petersen, Francye Phillips, Betsy and Joseph Pistone, Paula Poole, Erika Prosper, Kay Ray, Shannon Riley, Laura Cate Roberts, Aleigh Sanchez, Julia Sanders, Whitney Schaap, Daphne Scott, Tracey Smith, Laurie Smith, Bryan Snowden, Laura Sparks, Madison Stahl, Cheylo Steele, Sally Stephenson, Ariana Straughan, Enedelia Straughan, Sully Strohmeyer, Sharon Strong, Bettie Taylor, Sheryl and Thomas Thompson, Lyndon Todd,

Kay Tomlinson, Karen Torres, Lorena Trevino, Miranda Tubilla, Victoria Walker, Morgan Walton, Alex Waltrip, Pat Watson, Peggy Weed, Miranda Welborn, Tracey Welborn, and Hannah Wofford.

Thank you for following along and being a part of my journey. I had so much fun writing The Brew each week to keep you up to speed. I hope that we are able to share iced americanos and espresso martinis forever!

And last but certainly not least, thank you, my readers. I am *honored* that you selected *Mr. Americano* to add to your bookshelf. I hope you found a friend in Margaret, and always remember *there is a reason for every season, and the best is yet to come.*

XOXO

CPSIA information can be obtained
at www.ICGtesting.com
Printed in the USA
LVHW020149170323
741833LV00003B/109/J